CAD Demonstration Drawings

Paul Clarke

First Edition, May 2018

ISBN 978-0692119693

Published in the United States of America

Preface

Overview and Features

Designed for introductory CAD users, *CAD Demonstration Drawings* begins with the most basic concepts and tools and then progressively builds upon those concepts and tools with each successive assignment. The progressive and interconnected design of the assignments helps students master the most basic skills and incrementally learn more advanced tools and techniques with each new drawing. The assignments include real-world examples from diverse industries including architecture, engineering, landscape, mechanical, and interior design. Each drawing assignment begins with an introduction followed by suggested steps for completing the assignment. Specific commands appear in CAPS to aid quick entry at the command line. Occasionally the assignments end with questions which test students understanding and challenge them to explore concepts in greater depth. Each drawing has a corresponding demonstration video that takes students through the assignment step-by-step. The demonstration videos are available at the website: CADdemos.com

Dedication and Acknowledgements

CAD Demonstration Drawings was created for and is dedicated to all students who are and will make the world a better place one design at a time. The author offers his appreciation and thanks to all past students and present colleagues for their contributions to this work.

Demonstration Videos

Demonstrations videos for each drawing assignment are available through the following web site: CADdemos.com

Contents

Patterns

Introduction

Patterns are an important part of many design fields, including architecture, landscape, jewelry, and interior design. In this assignment, you will use the LINE command to create 16 different patterns, including 8 patterns of your own design. The Grid, Snap, and Polar Tracking buttons on the Status Bar are helpful features for creating these patterns in the drawing area.

Suggested Steps

1) Open a new file using the default *acad.dwt* template file

2) Turn on GRIDMODE, SNAPMODE, and Polar Tracking from the Status Bar (everything else off)

3) Use the LINE command to create a 10 x 10 square and 16 interior squares

4) Use the LINE command to draw the 8 patterns shown below

5) Use the LINE command to *create your own patterns* in the 8 bottom squares

6) Save your work as *PatternsXX.dwg* where *XX* is your initials

Bookshelf

<u>Introduction</u>

Most objects in the built environment are designed primarily with lines. In this assignment, you will use the LINE command to create a bookshelf while experimenting with the SNAPMODE and GRIDMODE in the ON and OFF positions. At this point, we are mainly concerned with using these commands and not making a realistic bookshelf to an accurate size or scale.

<u>Suggested Steps</u>

1) Open a new file using the default *acad.dwt* template file

2) Turn off everything on the Status Bar except GRIDMODE and SNAPMODE
   Tip: the F7 and F8 Function Keys toggle the Grid and Snap ON and OFF

3) Use the LINE command to create the bookshelf shown below (don't worry about size or scale yet)
   Tip: Don't worry about size or scale yet, but do keep your drawing proportional in size

4) Turn the SNAPMODE ON and OFF as needed while drawing items on the bookshelf
   Tip: Use the spacebar or enter keys to finish one line and repeat another line for speed

5) *Create your own* items on the bookshelf – be creative and have fun!

6) Save your work as *BookshelfXX.dwg* where *XX* is your initials

myPhone

<u>Introduction</u>

In this assignment you will create two phones using the ZOOM, RECTANG and CIRCLE commands. You will also learn about the Coordinate Display and how to use it while creating drawings.

<u>*Suggested Steps*</u>

1) Open a NEW drawing using the default acad.dwt Drawing Template file.

2) Use the ZOOM command with the All option to center the grid and display the entire drawing area on the screen. This can quickly be done at the command line using the command alias of "Z" for Zoom and "A" for All. The keystrokes would be Z<Enter> A<Enter> or the shortened Z←A← where "←" represents the "Enter" key on the keyboard. ZOOM All is used extensively in future assignments.

3) Set the SNAP to 0.25 and the GRID to 1 and turn them ON (Dynamic Input is on by default).

4) Turn on the Coordinate Display. The Coordinate Display by default does not show up on the Status Bar. To turn on the Coordinate Display pick the *Customization* button on the far-right end of the Status Bar and then pick *Coordinates* from the top of the menu. The Coordinate Display, positioned on the left side of the Status Bar, displays the X, Y, Z coordinates of the crosshairs at any location in the drawing area. AutoCAD uses the Cartesian coordinate system to record points based on their distance from the origin. The origin, in the lower left corner of the screen, has X, Y, and Z coordinates of 0,0,0 respectively. Coordinates based on the 0,0,0 origin are called absolute coordinates. As you move the crosshair in the drawing area you will see the X and Y coordinates change rapidly to display the changing location. Note that the Z coordinate does not change yet because we are working with a two-dimensional drawing.

5) Create the front view of a phone with a width of 2.5 and a height of 5 using the RECTANG command and picking the lower left and upper right corners of the rectangle.

6) Use the RECTANG command to create a 2 by 3.5 screen that begins 0.5 from the top edge. The RECTANG command can also be invoked through the Rectangle button in top right corner of the Draw panel on the Ribbon.

7) Draw the round button using the CIRCLE command. The center of the button is 0.5 from the bottom edge of the phone, and the button has a diameter of 0.5.

8) Draw your own phone on the right.
Save your work as *myPhoneXX.dwg* where *XX* is your initials.

Door

<u>Introduction</u>

The front doors on homes serve as entryways for guests, checkpoints for visitors and barriers for strangers. In this assignment, you will begin to design an entry door that provides security, functionality, and an attractive design. In the process, you will learn more about the UNITS, LIMITS, SNAP, GRID, ZOOM, and RECTANG commands.

<u>Suggested Steps</u>

1) Open a new file using the *acad.dwt* template file and then change the UNITS and LIMITS as follows:

UNITS (Length):	Type: Architectural	Precision: 0'-0"
LIMITS:	Lower left: 0'-0",0'-0"	Upper right: 3'-0",6'-8"

Note that the drawing limits are being set to be same size as the door. We are doing this to explore how the limits work in conjunction with ZOOM command and the SNAP and GRID settings.

2) Set the GRID to 1' and the SNAP to 2" and the GRIDDISPLAY to 0. Architectural units require distances to be entered in feet and inches. When entering feet at the command line in AutoCAD be sure to include an apostrophe (') for the foot mark or AutoCAD will default to inches. Consider turning everything off at the status bar except SNAP and GRID (Dynamic Input is on by default).

3) Use the ZOOM All command to display the drawing limits in the visible area of the drawing screen. Then use ZOOM <real time> to make the drawing limits display at a smaller scale by dragging down (-).

4) Use the RECTANG command to draw a door that is 3' wide and 6' 8" tall. The two bottom panels are 10" by 2' and start 8" from the bottom and 6" from the sides of the door. The two top panels are 10" by 3' and start 6" from the top of the door.
With the SNAP, GRID, and Dynamic Input turned on you can complete these objects without keying in any distances.

5) Use the CIRCLE command to create a doorknob with a center point 4" from the edge and a diameter of 2-1/2". Experiment with the ZOOM command options from the navigation bar and command line.

6) Draw your own door design on the right, but make sure the overall size remains 3' by 6'8". And then save your work as *DoorXX.dwg* where *XX* is your initials.

Site

Introduction

Landscape design for an existing home begins by creating a site plan and drafting the existing structure, hardscape, and landscape. The design work for new landscape features occurs later in the process. In this project you complete an upgraded landscape design for an existing home. The first step is to draw the site. You will use the UNITS, LIMITS, AREA and several coordinate entry methods to create the site. Precision is important in this assignment – follow the steps closely and type in the commands carefully.

Suggested Steps

1) Open a new drawing using the *acad.dwt* template and then change the UNITS and LIMITS as follows:

UNITS (Length):	Type: Engineering	Precision: 0'-0"
LIMITS:	Lower left: 0'-0", 0'-0"	Upper right: 340'-0", 220'-0"

2) Use the ZOOM ALL command to display the drawing limits in the visible area of the drawing screen.

3) Use the *Customization* button at the right end of the Status Bar to turn on *Dynamic Input* (note it is NOT displayed in the Status Bar by default). Then turn off Dynamic Input and everything else at the Status Bar.

4) Create the site boundary using the POLYLINE command and the following coordinate entry methods:

Line 1 (Absolute Method): 150',30' <Enter>
199',17'-6" <Enter>
Line 2 (Relative Method): @15'-9",34'-5" <Enter>
Line 3 (Polar Method): @146'-9"<85 <Enter>
Line 4 (Relative Method): @-94'-5",0 <Enter>
Line 5 (Close): C <Enter>

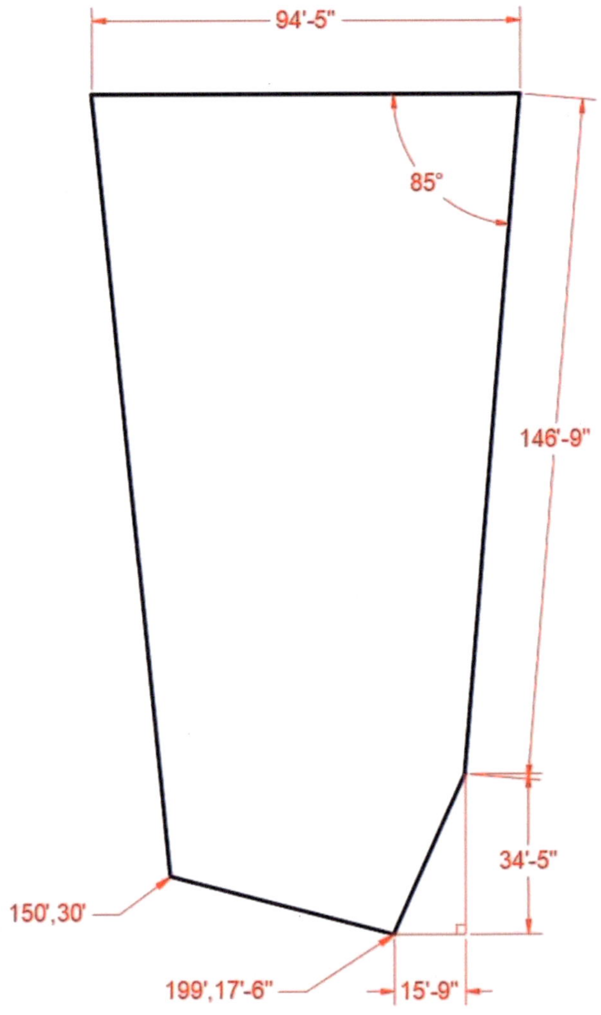

5) Check the area of your site using the AREA command or other measuring tools. The area of this site should be 13,470.55 square feet.

6) Save your work as *SiteXX.dwg* where *XX* is your initials (Note you do NOT need to show the dimensions).

Structure

Introduction

The next step in our landscape design is to draw the existing home on the site. An outline of the structure is all the detail needed, as our focus is on the landscape features. The POLYLINE, SNAP, GRID, ZOOM, and PAN commands will be helpful in creating the structure and moving around the drawing area. The TIME, AREA, and Coordinate Display tools will be helpful in checking our work.

Getting Started

Begin by opening the drawing file *SiteXX.dwg* previously created. Reset the timer using the TIME command.

Set the SNAP and GRID as follows: SNAP: 6" GRID: 10'

Turn on the SNAPMODE, GRIDMODE, and Polar Tracking at the Status Bar. Use the ZOOM and PAN commands to display the top portion of the site where the structure is located.

Picking Distances

Create the structure using the POLYLINE command. The first point can be entered using the absolute coordinate: 210',170'. The remaining points can be picked without entering distances using the Snap Grid. The Visual Grid and Polar Tracking assist in picking the correct distances shown below.

Checking Measurements

You can check the area of the structure using the AREA command or other measuring tools. The area of the house drawing should be 3208.5 square feet.

Using the Coordinate Display, double check to ensure the first point of the structure began at exactly 210',170'.

Check the elapsed timer using the TIME command to see how long you have spent on the drawing.

Finishing-up

Save your work as *StructureXX.dwg* where *XX* represents your initials (Note you do not need to show dimensions).

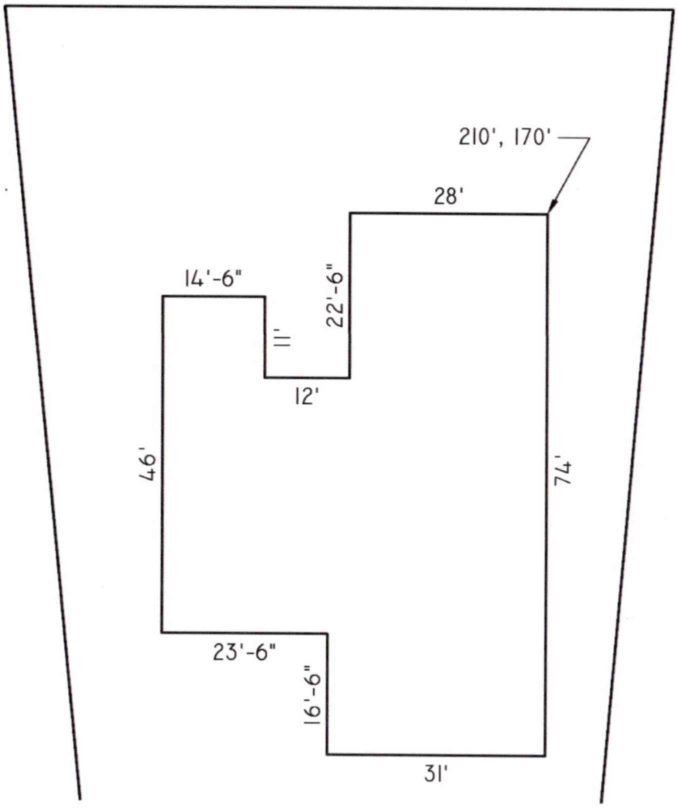

LandscapeLayers

Introduction

Different companies and industries have their own standards for layers. Each layer assigns a color, linetype, and lineweight to a group of similar features. In this assignment we will create and apply layers to the Structure drawing previously created.

Suggested Steps

1) Open the *StructureXX.dwg* file and create new layers with the names, colors, linetypes, and lineweights shown below. The Layer Properties Manager palette can be accessed through the Layer Properties button on the Ribbon or by keying in LAYER at the command line.

S...	Name	O...	Fre...	L...	Color	Linetype	Lineweight	Trans
	0				white	Continuous	Default	0
	Brick				12	Continuous	0.25 mm	0
	Concrete				white	Continuous	0.30 mm	0
	Flagstone				42	Continuous	0.25 mm	0
	Hatch				white	Continuous	Default	0
	PropertyLine				magenta	PHANTOM	0.70 mm	0
	Rosebushes				green	Continuous	0.25 mm	0
	RR Ties				17	Continuous	0.50 mm	0
	Structure				255	Continuous	0.50 mm	0
	Trees				94	Continuous	0.40 mm	0

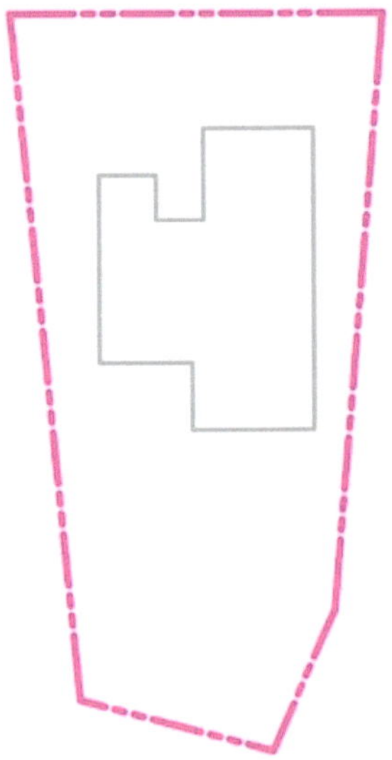

2) Apply the *Structure* and *PropertyLine* layers to the related drawing elements.

3) Turn on the Lineweight Display by picking the *Customization* button on the right side of the Status Bar and selecting *LineWeight*. The LWDISPLAY button is now visible on the Status Bar and you may turn it on and off at the Status Bar or by keying in LWDISPLAY and then ON or OFF.

4) Set the Linetype Scale (LTS). The LTS is equal to the drawing scale factor divided by two. The scale factor for this drawing is 240, therefore the LTS is 120. Notice what happens to the PHANTOM Linetype in the PropertLine layer when the LTS is changed from 1 to 120. What happens and why?

5) Save your drawing as *LandscapeLayersXX.dwg* where *XX* is your initials.

Door2

Introduction

In this assignment we add layers, chamfers, fillets to our Door drawing. Layers allow us to assign and consistently apply colors, lineweights, and linetypes to objects that are similar. In drawing a house elevation for example, we might want to have separate layers for the doors, windows, fixtures, dimensions, borders, text, and other elements of the drawing. We will use the LAYER, FILLET, CHAMFER, ZOOM, and PAN commands to complete this assignment.

Suggested Steps

1) Open the *DoorXX.dwg* file that contains your door drawing.

2) Add two new layers using the LAYER command to invoke the Layer Properties Manager palette. One of the new layers will be named *Doors* and the other will be named *Fixtures*. The Doors layer should be assigned the cyan color and the Fixtures layer should be assigned a red color. The *Linetype* for both layers is *Continuous.* The *Lineweight* for *Doors* is 0.25mm and the *Lineweight* for *Fixtures* is 0.20mm.

3) Put the objects in the drawing on the proper layers. All objects in the drawing are currently on the default "0" layer. You can easily put them on the proper layers by selecting the object you would like to be on the *Doors* layer and then picking *Doors* from the Layer list box on the ribbon. Repeat this procedure for the doorknob, and put it on the *Fixtures* layer.

4) Use the FILLET command to create 1/8" fillets for each of the four corners of the door. These fillets are small - the ZOOM command with the Window option will help you view them.

5) Add chamfers to all four panels using the CHAMFER command with a Distance 1" for both edges.

6) Use the RECTANG command with the Chamfer option to quickly create four interior panels that are 1" from the existing panels. You will want to change the SNAP to 1" to make this task easier.

7) Add layers to the door you created on the right and consider adding fillets and chamfers as needed.

8) Save your work as *Door2XX.dwg* where *XX* is your initials.

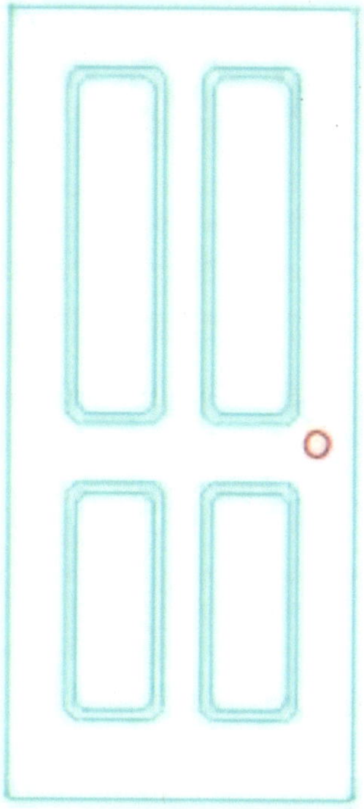

myPhone2

Introduction

In this assignment we will add layers and fillets to the myPhone. The layers will include specific colors, lineweights, and linetypes that will be applied in the next assignment. Putting fillets on products eliminates sharp edges thereby reducing the chance of injury from products that come in contact with people. We will use the LAYER, FILLET and ZOOM commands to complete this assignment.

Suggested Steps

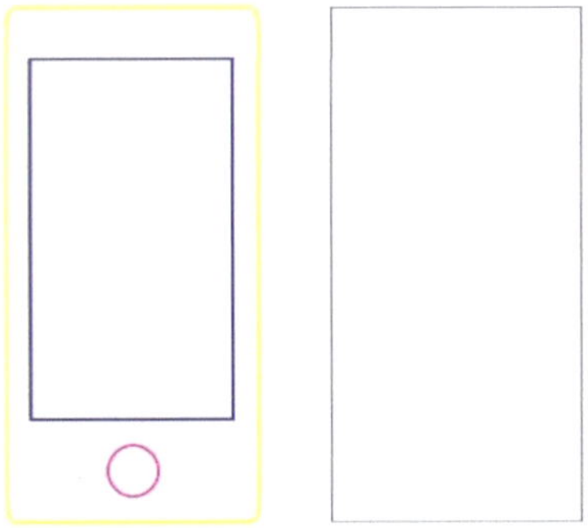

1) Open the drawing file *myPhoneXX.dwg*

2) Open the *Layers Property Manager* palette by keying LAYER at the command line or picking the *Layer Properties* button from the Ribbon.

3) Create layers with Names, Colors, Linetypes, and Lineweights shown below:

S...	Name	O...	Fre...	L...	Color	Linetype	Lineweight
	0				white	Continuous	Default
	Button				magenta	Continuous	0.50 mm
	Center				red	CENTER2	0.20 mm
	Hidden				magenta	HIDDEN	0.30 mm
✓	Object				yellow	Continuous	0.50 mm
	Screen				blue	Continuous	0.50 mm
	xLine				white	Continuous	Default

4) Apply the Button, Screen, and Object layers to your phone by selecting the feature you want and picking the layer from the Layer list box on the Ribbon. The button goes on the Button layer, the screen goes on the Screen layer, and the phone outline goes on the Object layer.

5) Turn on the Lineweight Display by picking the *Customization* button on the right side of the Status Bar and selecting *LineWeight.* The LWDISPLAY button is now visible on the Status Bar and you may turn it on and off at the Status Bar or by keying in LWDISPLAY and then ON or OFF.

6) Add fillets to the four corners of the phone using the FILLET command with a radius of 0.125

7) Experiment with the *Center* and *Hidden* layers by drawing simple objects and changing the LTS. What happens to the objects in these layers when the LTS gets bigger and smaller?

8) Apply layers to your phone on the right, and fillets and chamfers as needed. Save your work as *myPhone2XX.dwg* where *XX* is your initials.

myPhoneMV

Introduction

In this assignment you will create a simple multiview drawing for the myPhone2 using orthographic projection principles and construction aids. The multiview drawing will include front, top and right-side views based on ASME projection standards. These three regular views form the bases of a multiview drawing. We will use and practice applying the LAYERS, PAN, ZOOM, SNAP, XLINE and ARC commands.

Suggested Steps

1) Open the *myPhone2XX.dwg* file previously created. Remember this drawing already has layers with Names, Colors, Linetypes, and Lineweights.

2) Begin by deleting the myPhone on the righthand side that you designed previously.

3) Use the PAN and ZOOM real time to position the Front view of the myPhone in the lower left corner of the drawing area.

4) Project the top view using vertical construction lines - the XLINE command with *Ver* option works well. The myPhone has a thickness of 0.25 and the screen and button both have a thickness of 0.0625. Changing the SNAP to 0.0625 allows the screen and button to be drawn in the top view without keying in any values. The button can be drawn using the ARC command with the default 3-Point Arc. Change the Linetype Scale (LTS) to 0.5 and observe how the Hidden line changes.

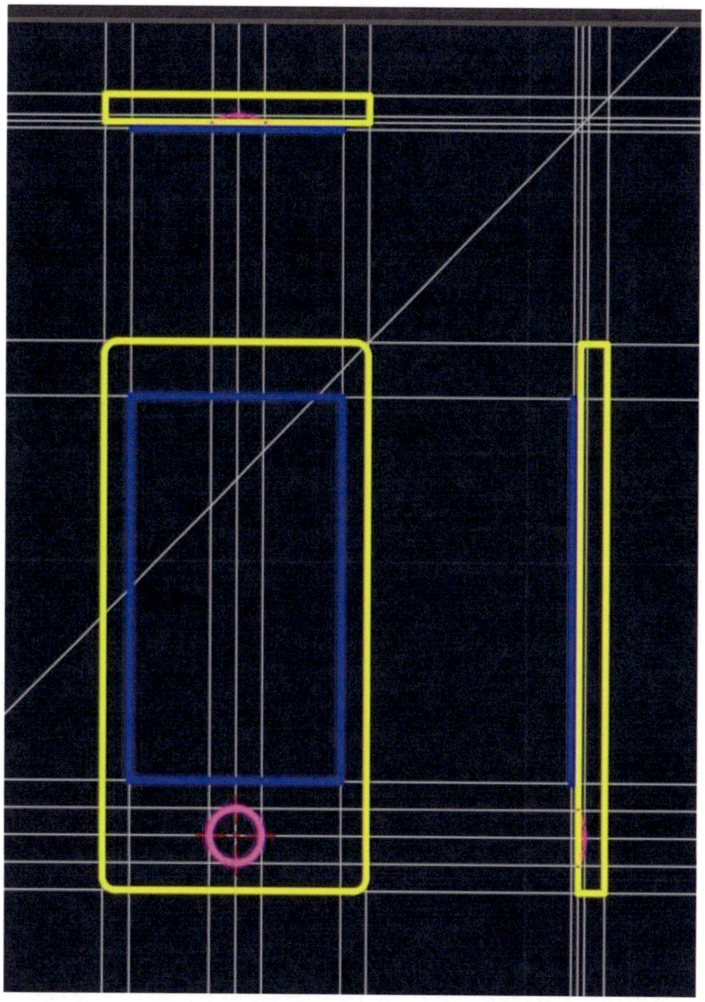

5) Project the right side view. This can be done by projecting the width of the right side view over and down from the top view using a miter line with a 45 degree angle (Angular option of the XLINE), and projecting the height of the Right Side view over from the Front view (Horizontal option of the XLINE).

6) Draw the two center lines for the button in the front view on the *Center* layer. Check to make sure all objects are on the correct layer and that the linetypes display properly. Turn off the xLine layer.

7) Save your work as *myPhoneMV-XX.dwg* where *XX* is your initials.

TemplateEV

<u>Introduction</u>

Templates have various settings preset to save time and improve consistency. In this assignment we will create a template file with basic settings such as units, drawing area (limits), layers, linetype scale, snap, and grid display. We will use this template in future assignments to create a home elevation drawing.

<u>Suggested Steps</u>

1) Open a new file using the default *acad.dwt* template file and set the UNITS and LIMITS as follows:
   - UNITS (Length) to *Architectural* with a precision of 0'-0"
   - LIMITS for a B-size sheet (11x17) with a scale of ¼" = 1'

   This can be done at the command line: LIMITS←←68',44'←

2) Create the LAYERs shown to the right.
Set the Linetype Scale: LTS←24← (Note LTS is ½ scale factor or 48/2=24).

3) Set the SNAP to 6" and the GRID to 1' and set the GRIDDISPLAY to 0. Note this is a system variable for grid behavior that eliminates adaptive grid and display grid beyond limits. This can also be done in the Drafting Settings dialog box.

S...	Name	O...	Fre...	L...	Color	Linetype	Lineweight
✓	0				white	Continuous	Default
	Border				white	Continuous	0.70 mm
	Center				magenta	CENTER	Default
	Dimensions				red	Continuous	Default
	Doors				cyan	Continuous	0.25 mm
	Fixtures				red	Continuous	0.20 mm
	Hatch				12	Continuous	0.09 mm
	Hidden				85	HIDDEN	0.15 mm
	Object				blue	Continuous	0.50 mm
	Text				red	Continuous	Default
	Title				green	Continuous	0.50 mm
	Viewport				yellow	PHANTO...	Default
	Windows				cyan	Continuous	Default

4) Do a ZOOM All (Z←A←) and observe how the drawing limits are reflected in the Grid Display.

5) Turn on Snap, Grid, Polar Tracking, Object Snap, and Object Snap Tracking at the Status Bar.

6) Use the STATUS command to check the status of the drawing settings.

7) Save the file as *TemplateEV-XX.dwt* where *XX* is your initials. Note the .dwt file extension ('t' as in template). The *Save Drawing As* dialog box will default to the template folder when the template file type is selected. You can browse to a folder of your choice to save the template file. After saving your template file a *Template Options* box appears allowing you to type a *Description* for the template.

8) Start a NEW drawing using the template file you just created and then answer the following questions. What happens to the name and file type after you open it? What changed and why?

LandTemp

Introduction

In this assignment you will create a template file that will eventually be used to print the Landscape drawing on a B-size sheet of paper from a Layout tab in Paper Space.

Suggested Steps

1) Open a new file using the default *acad.dwt* template file

2) Set the UNITS to Engineering with a Precision of 0'-0.00"

3) Calculate the limits given the following information:

Viewport Size (VS): 6.5"x10"

Scale: 1" = 20'

Scale Factor (SF) = 240 (there are 240 inches in 20 feet)

LIMITS = VS X SF = 6.5" X 240 = 1560" = 130' (1560"/12 inches per foot)

= 10" X 240 = 2400" = 200' (2400"/12 inches per foot)

4) Enter the limits in the model tab in model space: LIMITS←←130', 200'←

5) Set the SNAP to 1' and the GRID to 10'

6) Turn off the *Adaptive grid* and *Display grid beyond Limits* (GRIDDISPLAY to 0)

7) Do a ZOOM All (Z←A←) to display the entire drawing area on the screen

8) Create the following Layers

Name	Color	Linetype	Lineweight
Border	White	Continuous	.90mm
Text	Red	Continuous	.50mm
Vport	Yellow	Continuous	.30mm

9) Set the linetype scale: LTS← 120← (note that LTS = SF/2 = 240/2 = 120)

10) Create the following new text STYLEs

Name	Font	Height
Notes	Romans.shx	0.25"
Title	Romans.shx	0.5"

11) Check the status of the template file: STATUS←

12) Save the file as *LandTempXX.dwt* where *XX* is your initials

Deck

Introduction

You are helping your brother build an island or 'floating' deck. The deck framing is pressure treated 2"x6" lumber with no beams or in ground post footers. The posts will use the same 2"x6" material cut to size and resting on 4"x8" bricks. Keep in mind a 2"x6" is the nominal name of the lumber; the actual size is 1.5"x5.5" because of the finishing that removes more material. To protect the roots of a nearby avocado tree, none of the posts go into the ground - they all rest above ground on top of the bricks. To ensure the deck is stable and does not sag, your brother insists each interior 2"x6" framing member is 12" on center AND is supported by three posts. One end member must be less than 12" on center to maintain the overall 12' dimension required for the composite decking.

Suggested Steps

1) UNITS: Architectural, precision 0'-0 1/2"
2) LIMITS: 0,0 (lower left); 14',14' (upper right)
3) SNAP ½" and GRID 1'
4) GRIDDISPLAY to 0
5) ZOOM All (Z←A←)
6) LAYERs: Bricks (red), Framing (white), Posts (green)
7) Commands: RECTANG, ARRAY, MOVE, COPY
8) Save the file as *DeckXX.dwg* where *XX* is your initials

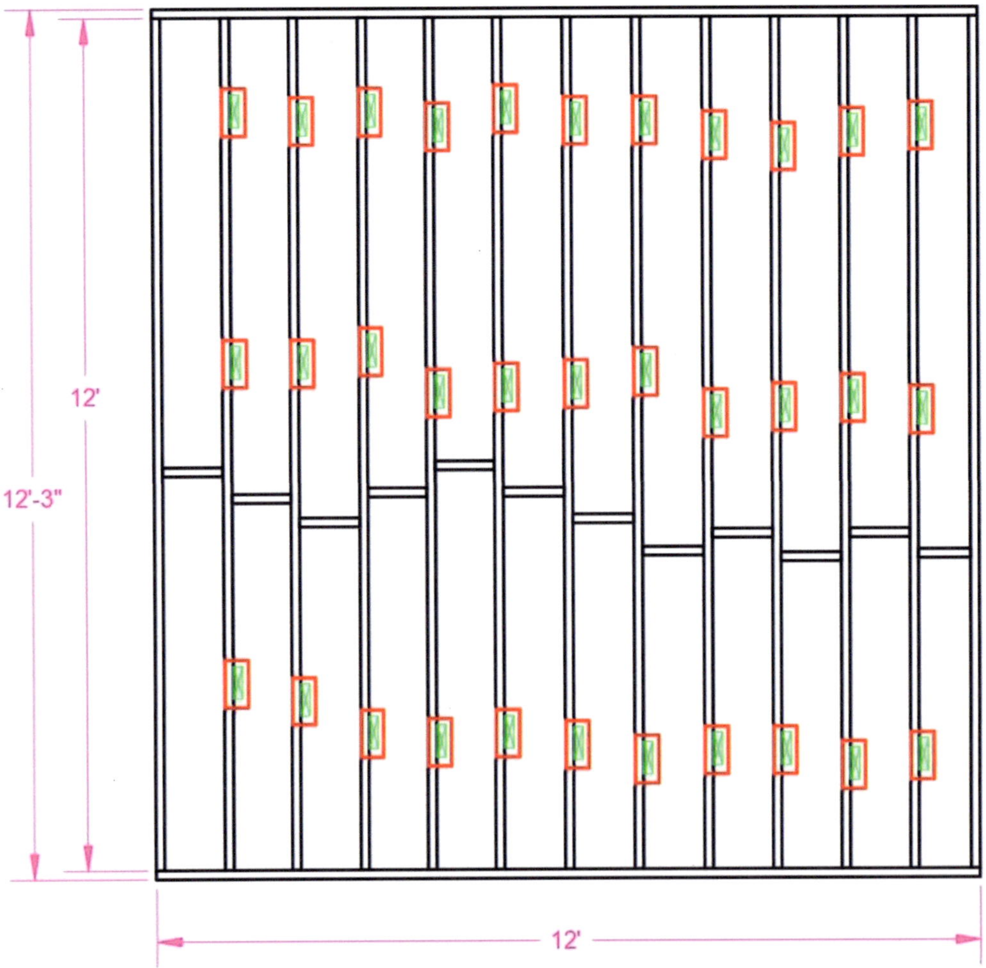

Classroom

<u>Introduction</u>

In this assignment we will create 24 chairs for a classroom layout using the ARRAY command.

<u>Suggested Steps</u>

1) Setup the drawing with the following settings:

UNITS: Architectural, Precision 0'0"

SNAP 1" and GRID 1'

ZOOM ALL: Z←A←

LIMITS: 0,0 (Lower left), 30',20' (Upper right)

GRIDDISPLAY: 0 (OFF)

Status Bar: SNAP, GRID, Dynamic Input

2) Draw a RECTANG around the drawing limits to represent the interior walls of the classroom.

3) Draw a 2' square chair with a 6" back support using the RECTANG command with 3" fillets on each corner. Begin the first chair 5' from the front and 5' from (bottom) side of the room.

4) ARRAY the chair with 6 columns at 4' spacing and 4 rows at 2',8" spacing.

5) Save your work as *ClassroomXX.dwg* where *XX* is your initials.

<u>Question</u>

The administration wants to squeeze more chairs into the classroom. Assuming there needs to be a 5' walkway around the front and sides of the room, how many chairs can be put into the classroom while still allowing students to safely get in and out?

myPhone3

<u>Introduction</u>

In this assignment you will modify your myPhone2 drawing using the PROPERTIES Palette and the ARC, SPLINE, MOVE, COPY, BREAK, and MIRROR commands.

<u>Suggested Steps</u>

1) Start by opening the file *myPhone2XX.dwg* created previously

2) Move the circular button from the center of the phone to the left .75" using the PROPERTIES Palette

3) COPY the button back to center and the right side of the phone.

4) Change the diameter of the center button from .5" to .625" using the PROPERTIES Palette.

5) COPY the phone to the left leaving a 1" space between the original phone. This can be done using the COPY command and keying in a Displacement of 3.5" or by picking points referencing the grid.

6) Put handles on both sides of the phone. This can be done by modifying the sides of the phone with a 3" BREAK using a first point 1" from the top and a second point 3" down from the first point. The break (gap) is then replaced with an ARC.

7) Customize your phone design on the right and MOVE it to be 1" from the middle phone.

8) Save your work as *myPhone3XX.dwg* where *XX* is your initials.

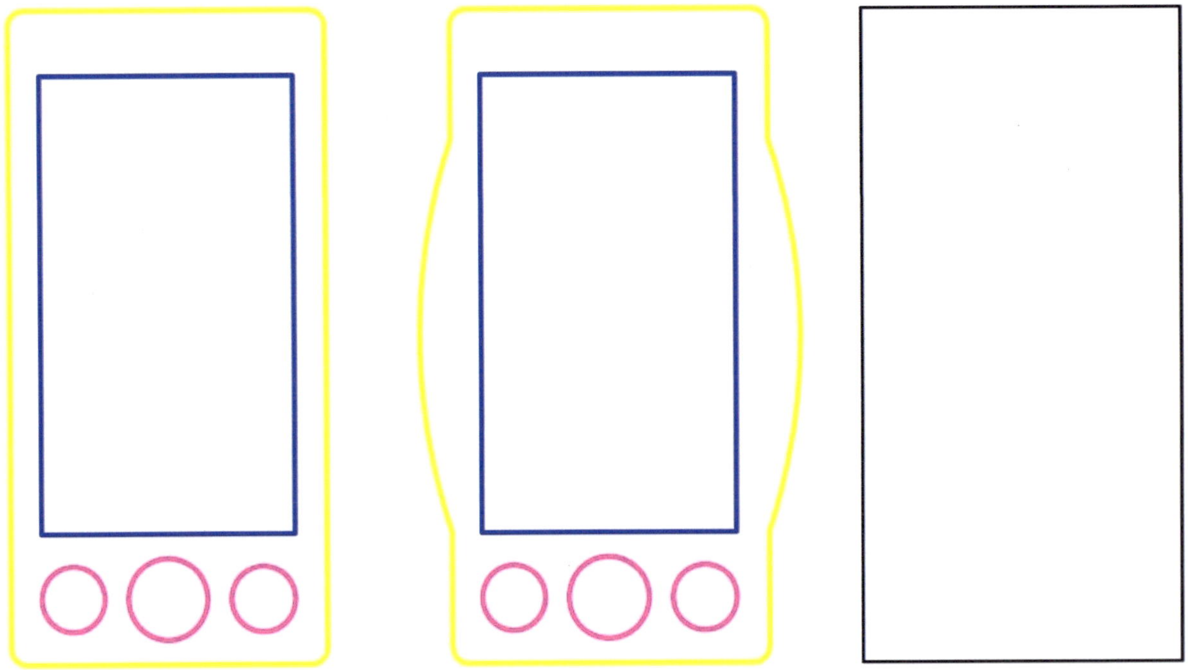

Wheel

<u>Introduction</u>

In this assignment you will create a wheel using the LINE, ARC, MIRROR and Polar ARRAY commands.

<u>Setup</u>

UNITS	Type: Decimal	Precision: 0
LIMITS	Lower left: 0,0	Upper right: 2500, 1800
SNAP	10	
GRID	100	
ZOOM All	Z←A←	

<u>Construction Tips</u>

Start by creating a circle with a diameter of 660 to represent the outer diameter of the tire. Then create the concentric circles to represent the rim, hub, and axel. Create the rim using the LINE, ARC and MIRROR commands. Array these two features separately using the Polar ARRAY command.

<u>Required</u>

Create another wheel on the right side and customize it to your own tastes.

Save your work as *WheelXX.dwg* where *XX* is your initials.

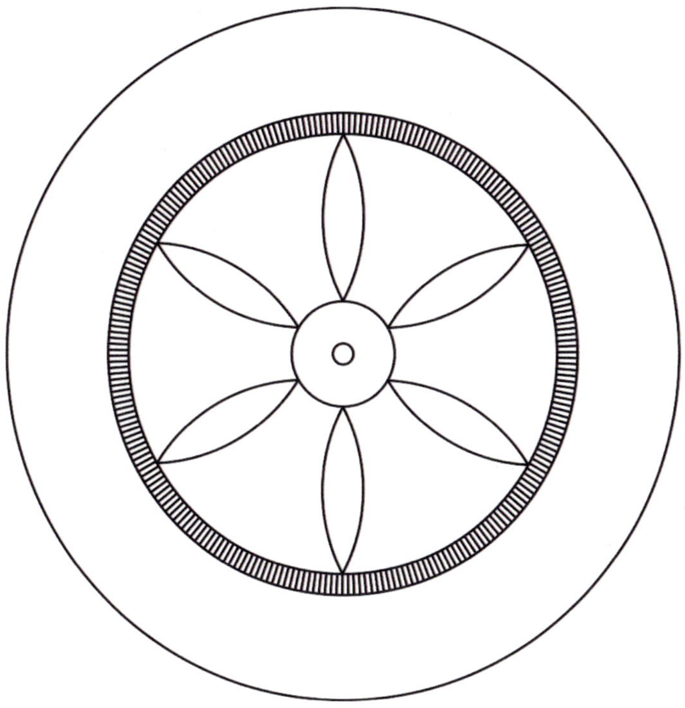

RoundTable

Introduction

A roommate got a “deal” on a table and custom chairs at a garage sale. She wants to see if the 10 foot diameter table will fit comfortably in your 20 foot by 20 foot basement with the 10 chairs around the table. Draw a quick representation of the room, table, and chairs to show her how it looks.

Setup

UNITS	Type: Architectural	Precision: 0’0”
LIMITS	Lower left: 0,0	Upper right: 20’,20’
SNAP	1”	
GRID	1’	
GRIDDISPLAY	0 (OFF)	
OSNAP	Midpoint	
Status Bar	SNAP, GRID, OSNAP	

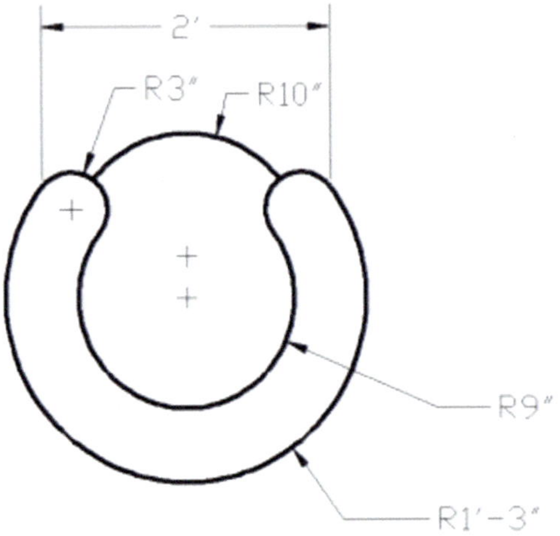

Commands & Tools

ZOOM (All & Window)
ARC
Grips
PROPERTIES Pallete
OFFSET
ARRAY (Polar)

Required

Save your work as *RoundTableXX.dwg* where *XX* is your initials.

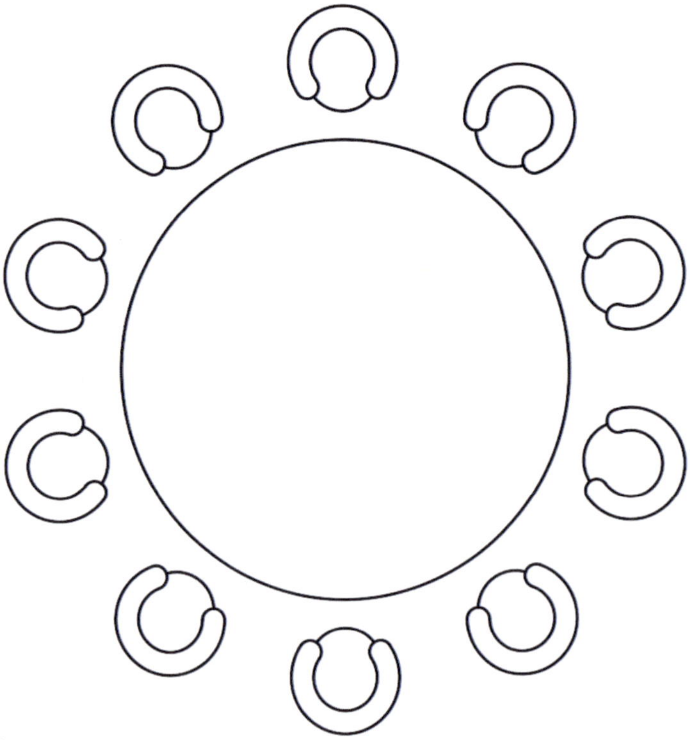

Additional Questions

Your roommate is having a big party and wants to know if 14 chairs will fit around the table?

She also wants to know if a second row of chairs will comfortably fit in the room?

Use the drawing model to answer these questions.

Snowflakes

Introduction

Symmetry is an important design principle. Objects that occur in nature, such as snowflakes, are often symmetrical and have reoccurring design patterns. The ARRAY and MIRROR commands work well for creating and recreating manmade and naturally occurring symmetrical designs.

Requirements

Create one of the six snowflakes shown below. Then create a second snowflake of your own design. Save both snowflakes in a single drawing file titled *SnowflakesXX.dwg* where *XX* is your initials.

Suggestions

Begin by drawing concentric circles based on the geometry of the snowflake. Use construction lines to divide the circles based on the number of sides needed. You might consider drawing half of one side and then using MIRROR to create the other half. Use the Polar ARRAY command to duplicate the lines and sides around the center point as needed.

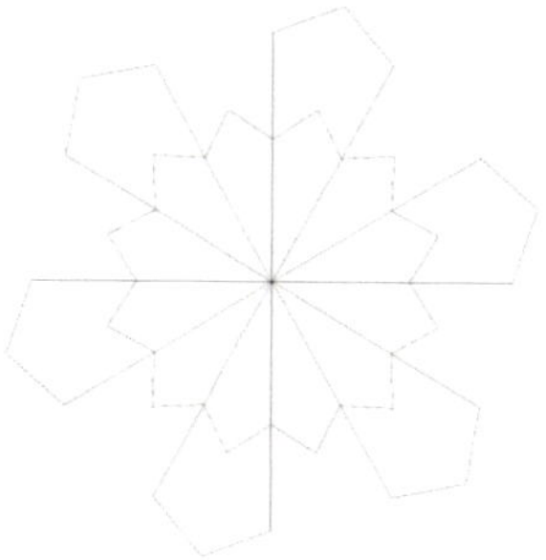

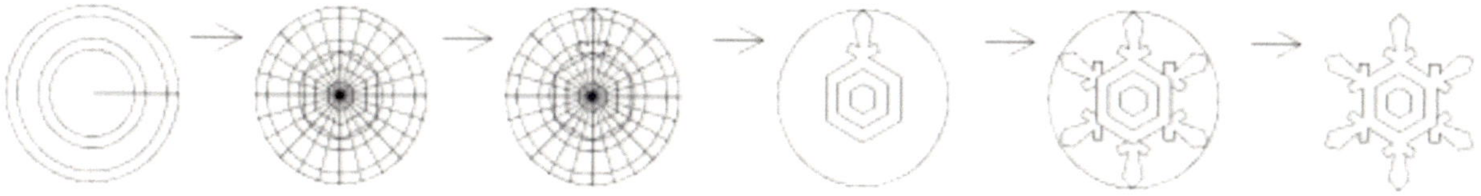

Concrete

Description

The concrete for a patio, sidewalk, and driveway will be added to the structure drawing. The EXPLODE, OFFSET, EXTEND, TRIM, HATCH and ROTATE commands will help create these concrete features. The Properties Palette will be used to determine hatch areas.

Suggested Steps

1) Open the *LandscapeLayersXX.dwg* file which contains the site and structure

2) Turn on the Display Grid, Polar Tracking, and Object Snap

3) Using the *Concrete* layer, create the existing concrete hardscape by a.) Drawing with the dimensions shown, b.) OFFSETing the site line at the North (top) end 5'6" below to create the sidewalk (EXPLODE the site polyline before offsetting), c.) EXTENDing the driveway to the side walk, and d.) TRIMing to clean up the driveway, sidewalk, and site intersections

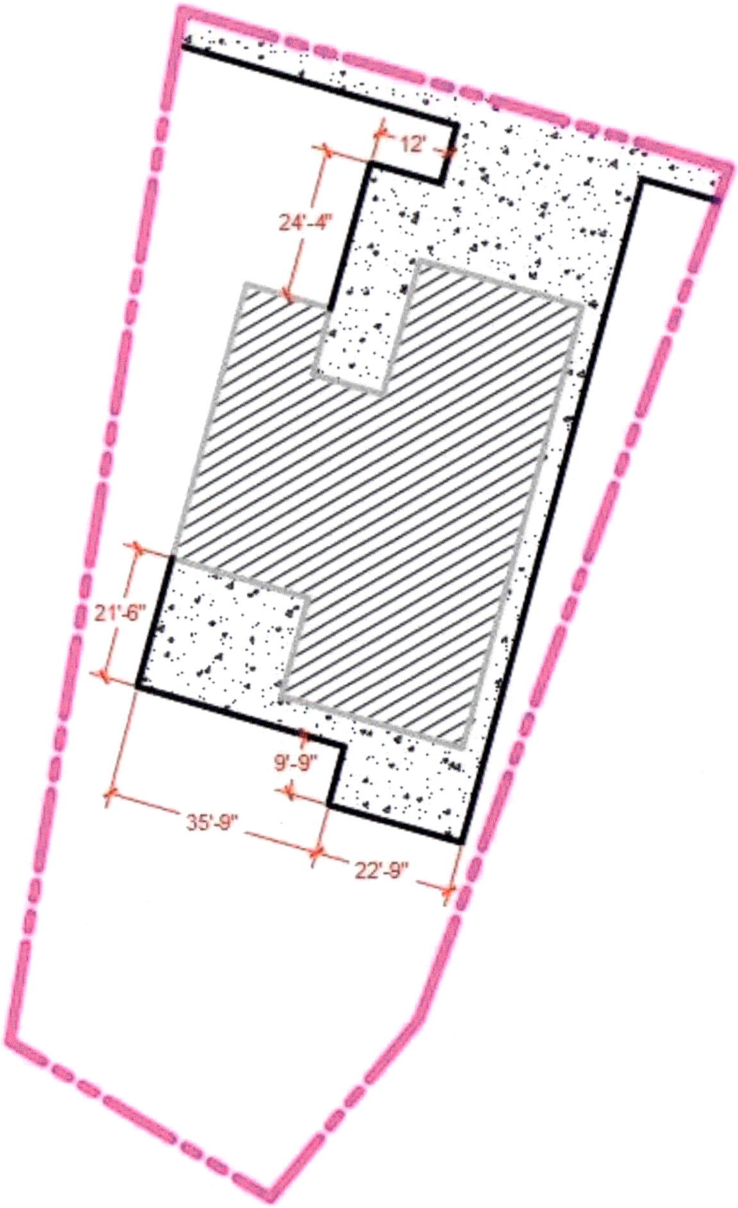

4) Using the *Hatch* layer HATCH the structure with ANSI31 (Scale=200) and the concrete with AR-CONC (Scale=12)

5) ROTATE the entire drawing minus 16 degrees using the top right corner as a base point

6) Save the file as *ConcreteXX.dwg* where *XX* is your initials

Checking Measurements

You can view the area of the structure and concrete by selecting the respective hatch patterns with the PROPERTIES palette open. The area of the structure is 3209 square feet and the area of the concrete is 2862 square feet.

Hardscape

Introduction

In this assignment we will add the existing hardscape to the backyard. The OFFSET, TRIM, PLINE, ARC, SPLINE, SPLINEDIT and HATCH commands will help in creating the brick and flagstone walkways, siding, and pond. We will also apply Object Snap to recreate the complex geometry required.

Getting Started

Open the *ConcreteXX.dwg* file previously created. Using reference geometry from the dimensions given below, create the existing brick walkway, siding, and flagstone areas around the pond. Apply LAYERs appropriately throughout the assignment.

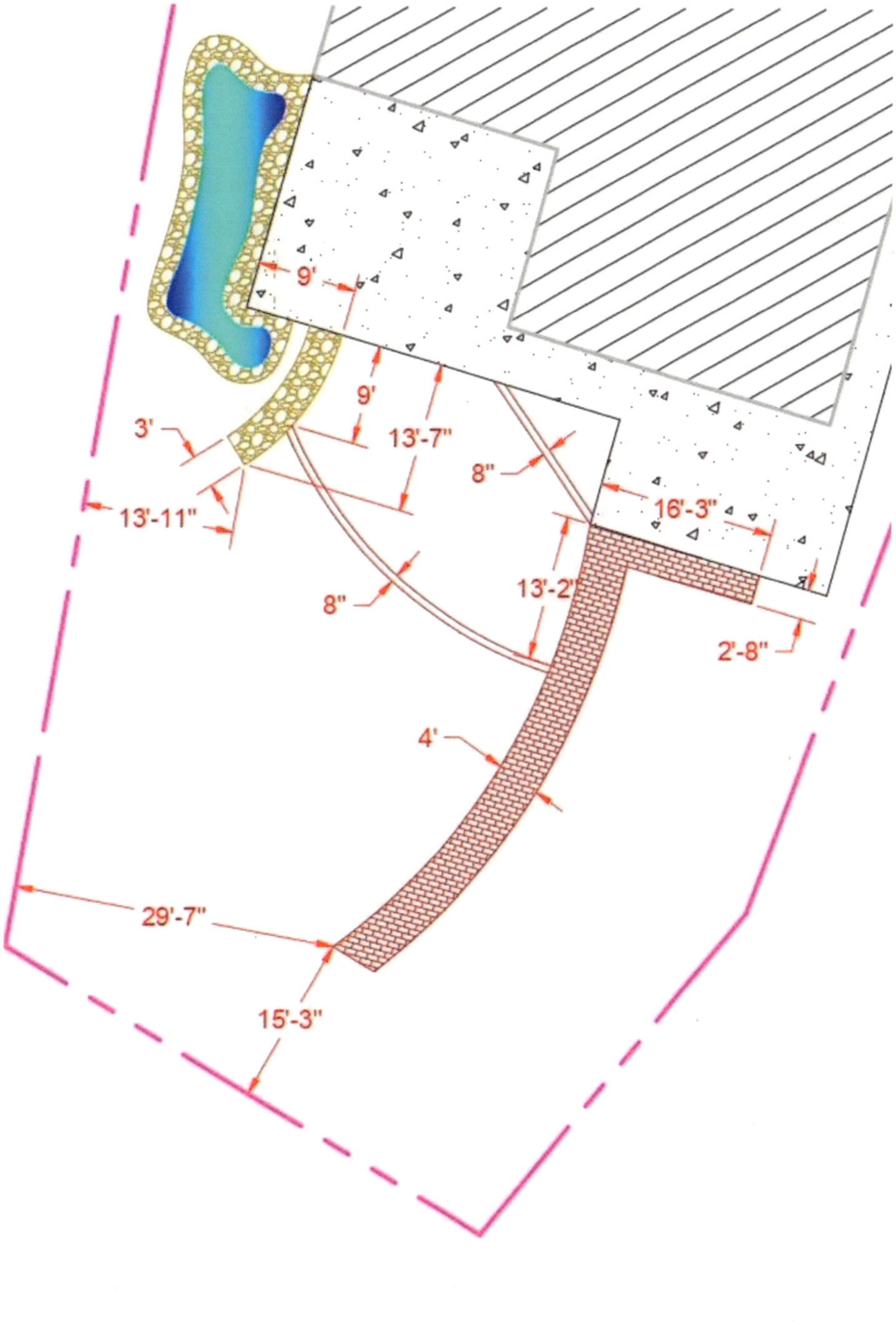

Status Bar

Grid Display

Object Snap

Object Snap Tracking

Running OSNAPs

Endpoint

Intersection

Extension

Helpful Commands

OFFSET

TRIM

ARC

PLINE

SPLINE

SPLINEDIT

HATCH

Finishing Up

Save the file as *HardscapeXX.dwg* where *XX* is your initials.

Bike

Introduction

In this assignment you will create a simple bike using various polar methods and object snap methods

Getting Started

Open a NEW drawing using the default *acad.dwt* template. Setup the drawing using the following drawing parameters:

UNITS	Type: Decimal	Precision: 0
LIMITS	Lower left: 0,0	Upper right: 2500,1800
ZOOM All	Z←A←	

OSNAP (Running Object Snaps): Endpoint, Center, Intersection, Extension

Status Bar: Polar Tracking, Object Snap, Object Snap Tracking

Step-by-Step Instructions

1.) Front Wheel (Circle with a 550 Diameter)	C←(pick point on left part of screen)D←550←
2.) Front Fork (Line 600 long at a 75° angle)	L←(pick center osnap)@600<75←
3.) Horizontal Frame (75 down from top of fork)	L←(acquire start point w/ osnap tracking)75←(polar tracking at 0° to right)600←
4.) Frame: Seat to Cranks (530 line at 255° angle)	@530<255
5.) Frame: Cranks to Forks	(Intersection osnap – first and second lines)←
6.) Frame: Cranks to Rear Wheel (500 horizontal line)	L←(Endpoint osnap)(polar tracking at 0°)500←
7.) Frame: Rear Wheel to Seat	(Endpoint object snap)←
8.) Rear Wheel (550 diameter circle)	C←(Endpoint object snap)D←550←

Finishing-up

Customize your bike wheels, frame, etc. to make it your own! Be creative and have fun!

Save your drawing as *BikeXX.dwg* where *XX* is your initials.

Rosegarden

Introduction

In this assignment we will add the existing rose garden to the backyard using the rectangular and polar ARRAY commands. Other useful commands include OFFSET, MIRROR, ROTATE, and MOVE.

The rose garden has two sections, each with 10 rosebushes, and a 2'9" walkway between the two sections. Railroad ties with a 7" plan width enclose each section.

Suggested Steps

1.) Open the *HardscapeXX.dwg* file previously created
2.) Draw the rose garden outside the site on the appropriate layers
3.) Use a 2'6" diameter reference CIRCLE and a polar ARRAY for the first rosebush
4.) Create the first section of rosebushes using a rectangular ARRAY with 2 columns and 5 rows with 4' spacing between the columns and 3' spacing between the rows
5.) Create the railroad tie using RECTANG and a 7" OFFSET
6.) MIRROR the first section using a 1'3" mirror line
7.) Check the angle of the top brick pathway and ROTATE the rose garden by the same value
8.) MOVE the rose garden into the backyard location as shown
9.) Save the file as *RosegardenXX.dwg* where *XX* is your initials

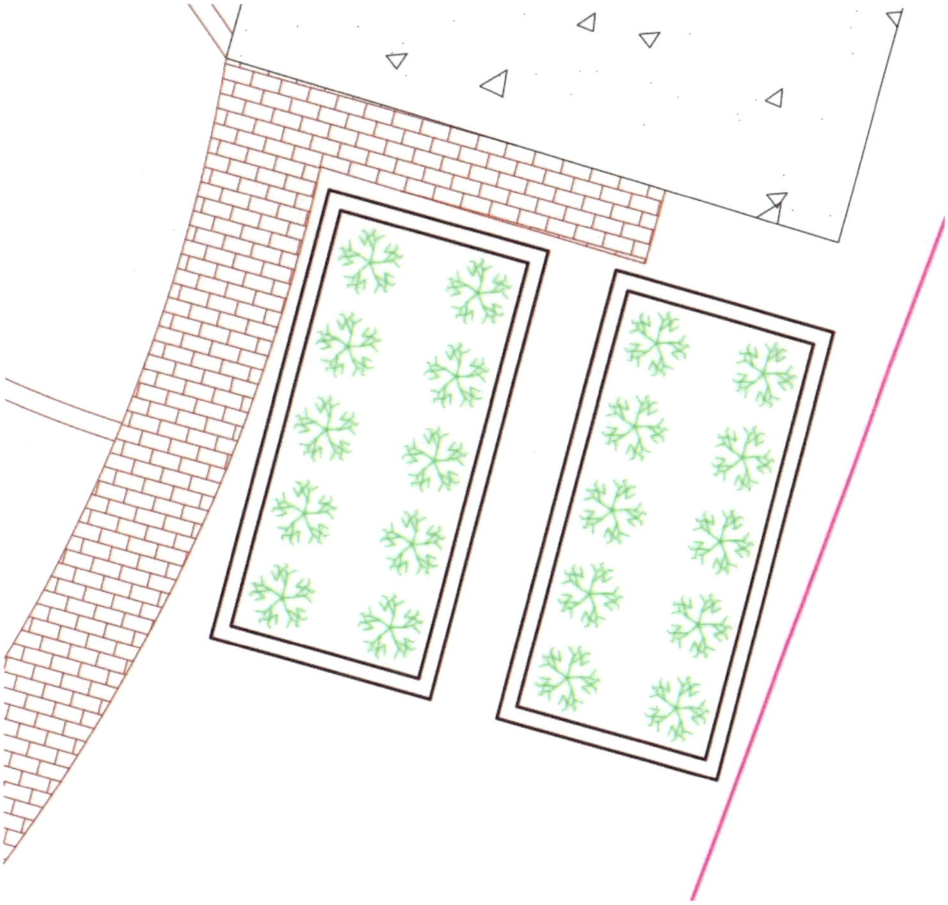

Trees

Introduction

In this assignment we will add the existing trees in the backyard using the OFFSET, EXTEND, BREAK, and CIRCLE commands. Other useful tools include Object Snap Tracking with the Extension and Perpendicular Object Snap modes.

Suggested Steps

1.) Open the *RosegardenXX.dwg* drawing file previously created
2.) Turn on Grid Display, Object Snap, Object Snap Tracking at the Status Bar
3.) Set the following Running Object Snaps: Endpoint, Center, and Extension
4.) Draw the necessary construction geometry using OFFSET and EXTEND
5.) Create the trees using the Extension and Perpendicular Object Snap and Tracking modes
6.) The CIRCLE and BREAK commands are helpful for the trees
7.) Save the file as *TreesXX.dwg* where *XX* is your initials

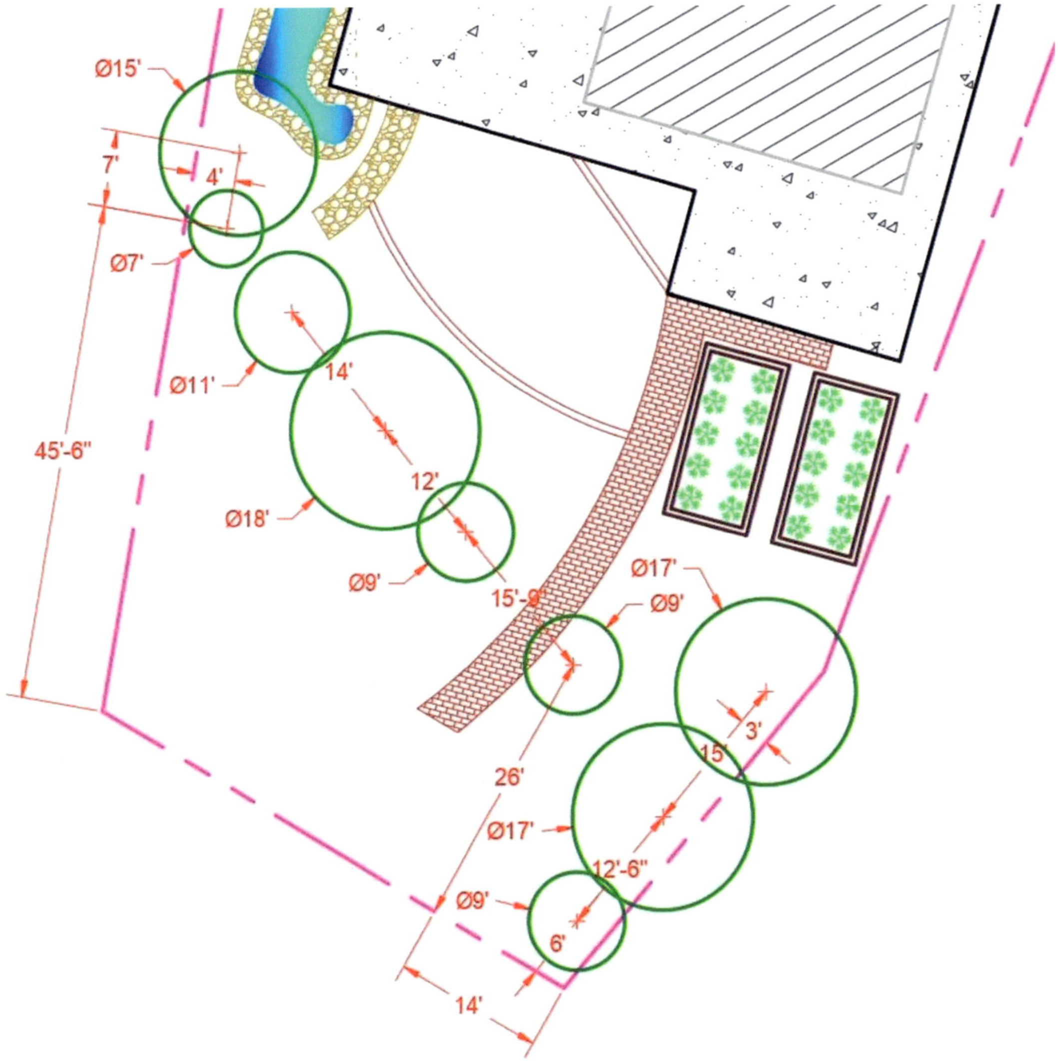

Elevation

Introduction

The front elevation of a residential home presents the view an observer would see from the street. The front elevation presents the curb appeal of a home, and is thus more important to clients and buyers than the side and back elevations. In this assignment you will create the front elevation for the home shown below.

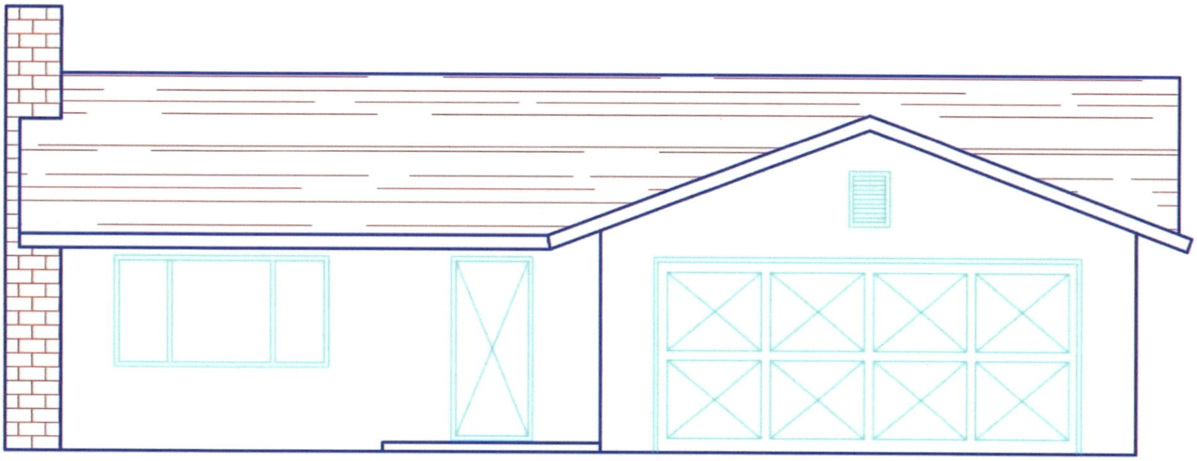

Suggested Steps

1) Open the *TemplateEV-XX.dwt* file (note this may have been saved as a .dwt or a .dwg file)

2) Save the file as *ElevationXX.dwg* where *XX* is your initials

3) Turn on Snap, Grid, Polar Tracking, Object Snap, and Object Snap Tracking at the Status Bar

4) Draw the house above using the appropriate layers for each feature

5) The residence is 42' from the left edge of the chimney to the right edge of the garage wall

6) The walls at the sides of the garage are 8' high and 20' apart

7) The angle of the garage roof is 20 degrees

8) Draw features to the following sizes: Window - 8' x 4' Front Door - 3' x 6'8" Garage Door - 16' x 7'

9) Each of the 8 panels on the garage door are 3'6" x 2'10" and 4" apart from each other

10) Use your best judgement in estimating size and location of features without measurements

11) HATCH the chimney with the *BRICK* pattern and the roof with the *AR-RROOF* pattern at a scale of 24

12) Save your file *ElevationXX.dwg* where *XX* is your initials

MechanicalTemp

Introduction

In this assignment we will begin creating a template file that will be used to print a mechanical drawing, such as myPhone3, from a Layout tab in Paper Space. A title block will be added in a future assignment.

Suggested Steps

1) Open the *acad.dwt* template file and set the UNITS to Decimal with a Precision of 0.000

2) Enter the lower left and upper right LIMITS: <1.000,1.375> <10.875,7.625>

3) Set the SNAP to .125, the GRID to .5, the GRIDDISPLAY to 0, and do a ZOOM ALL

4) Set the OSNAPS to Endpoint, Midpoint, and Intersection; turn on Snap, Grid, Polar Tracking and Object Snap at the Status Bar

5) Create these LAYERs
and set the LTS to .5

Name	Color	Lintype	Lineweight
Border	White	Continuous	.90mm
Text	White	Continuous	.30mm
Dims	Red	Continuous	.25mm
Vport	Cyan	Continuous	.20mm

6) Create the following new text STYLEs:
(Start with the *Standard* text style)

Name	Font	Height
Notes	Txt	.05”
Title	Arial	.20”

7) Rename Layout1 tab *A-Size Layout*, right click on *A-Size Layout*, select *Page Setup Manager*, then modify the *A-Size Layout* as follows:

- Printer/plotter Name: AutoCAD PDF
- Paper size: ANSI A (8.5 x11)
- What to plot: Layout

8) Rename Layout2 tab *B-Size Layout*, right click on *B-Size Layout*, select *Page Setup Manager*, then modify the *B-Size Layout* as follows:

- Printer/plotter Name: AutoCAD PDF
- Paper size: ANSI B (11 x 17)
- What to plot: Layout

9) Make a copy of the *A-Size Layout* tab, rename it *A-Size Portrait*, and modify it to have a *Portrait* drawing orientation in the *Page Setup Manager*

10) Add borders to the three layouts in Paper Space using the *Border* layer

11) Center and resize the viewports in the three layouts and put them on the *Vport* layer

12) Save the file as *MechanicalTempXX.dwg* where *XX* is your initials

TitleTemp

<u>Introduction</u>

In this assignment we will create a title block as part of the Mechanical Template. This file will be used to print a mechanical drawing, such as myPhone3, on A-size and B-size sheets of paper from Layout tabs in Paper Space. The OFFSET, BREAK, TRIM, and COPY commands are helpful for creating the titleblock lines, and the DTEXT and MTEXT commands are helpful for creating the titleblock text.

<u>Suggested Steps</u>

1) Open the *MechanicalTempXX.dwg* file previously created

2) Create the title block shown below in the Model tab (dimensions not required, for reference only)

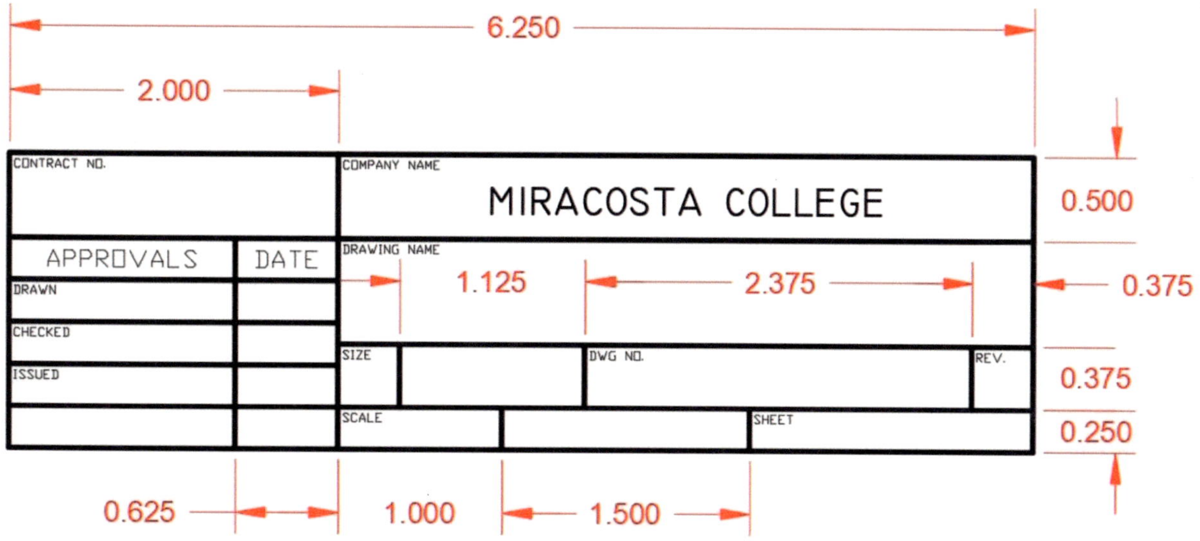

3) Copy the title block to the Clipboard with a Base Point of the lower right corner and then past the title block to the lower right corner of the borders in all three layout tabs

4) Delete the title block from the Model tab

5) Save the file as *TitleTempXX.dwg* where *XX* is your initials

<u>Construction Tips</u>

- ✓ Use the OFFSET, BREAK and TRIM commands to create the title block lines
- ✓ Use the *Text* layer and *Notes* text style to create the little text
- ✓ COPY the little text using a base point in the top left corner and then edit text
- ✓ Turn on and off Object Snap, Dynamic Input, etc. at the Status Bar as needed
- ✓ Use a diagonal line, Middle Center (MC) justification, and a midpoint object snap to create the "APPROVALS" and "DATE" text (note this text is twice the height of the *Notes* text)
- ✓ Use Multiline Text with MC justification to create the "MIRACOSTA COLLEGE" text

TitleblockEV

Introduction

In this assignment we will create a titleblock in model space for your elevation drawing. The OFFSET, BREAK, TRIM, and COPY commands are helpful for creating the titleblock lines, and the DTEXT and MTEXT commands are helpful for creating the titleblock text.

Suggested Steps

1) Begin by opening the *ElevationXX.dwg* drawing file

2) Create the following new Text STYLEs using the Standard text style as the starting point (not Annotative)
   - *TBtext* with 3" high *Txt* font
   - *TBentries* with 6" high *Stylus BT* font
   - *TBtitle* with 1' high *Stylus BT* font

3) Create the titleblock lines and border on the *Border* layer
   - The titleblock is 6'6" wide and 39'-6" tall
   - The horizontal entry lines begin ~4' from the bottom
   - The entry lines inside the titleblock are 1'6" apart

4) MOVE the titleblock into position

5) Create the three types of text in the titleblock
   - *TBtext* on the *Text* layer using Single Line TEXT
   - *TBentries* on the *Title* layer using Multiline MTEXT
   - *TBtitle* on the *Title* layer using Multiline MTEXT

6) FILLET the corners of the border and title block with a 6" radius

7) Save your work as *TitleblockEV-XX.dwg* where *XX* is your initials

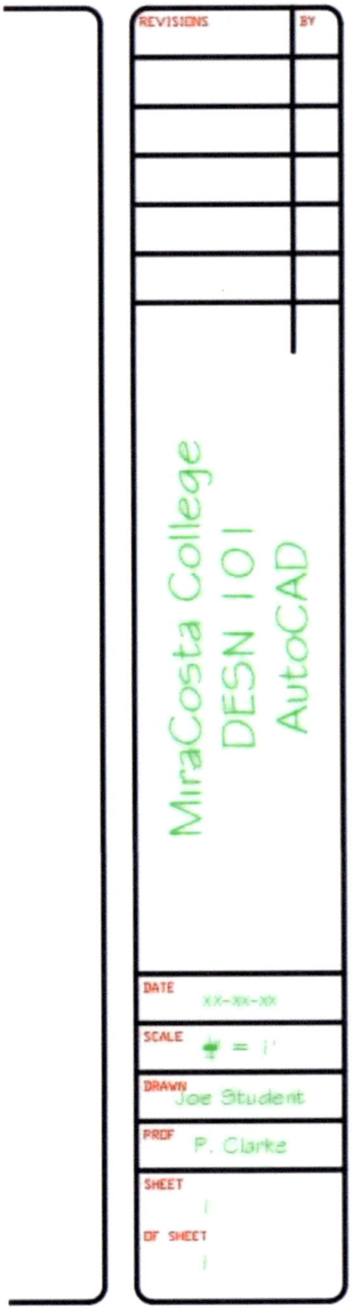

ParcelMap

Introduction

A client has provided you with part of a parcel map for a residential neighborhood that includes their lot. You need to produce an accurate drawing of site number 73 (22) in AutoCAD using the parcel map below. (Note this assignment is similar to the landscape site drawing, but more of a real-world example)

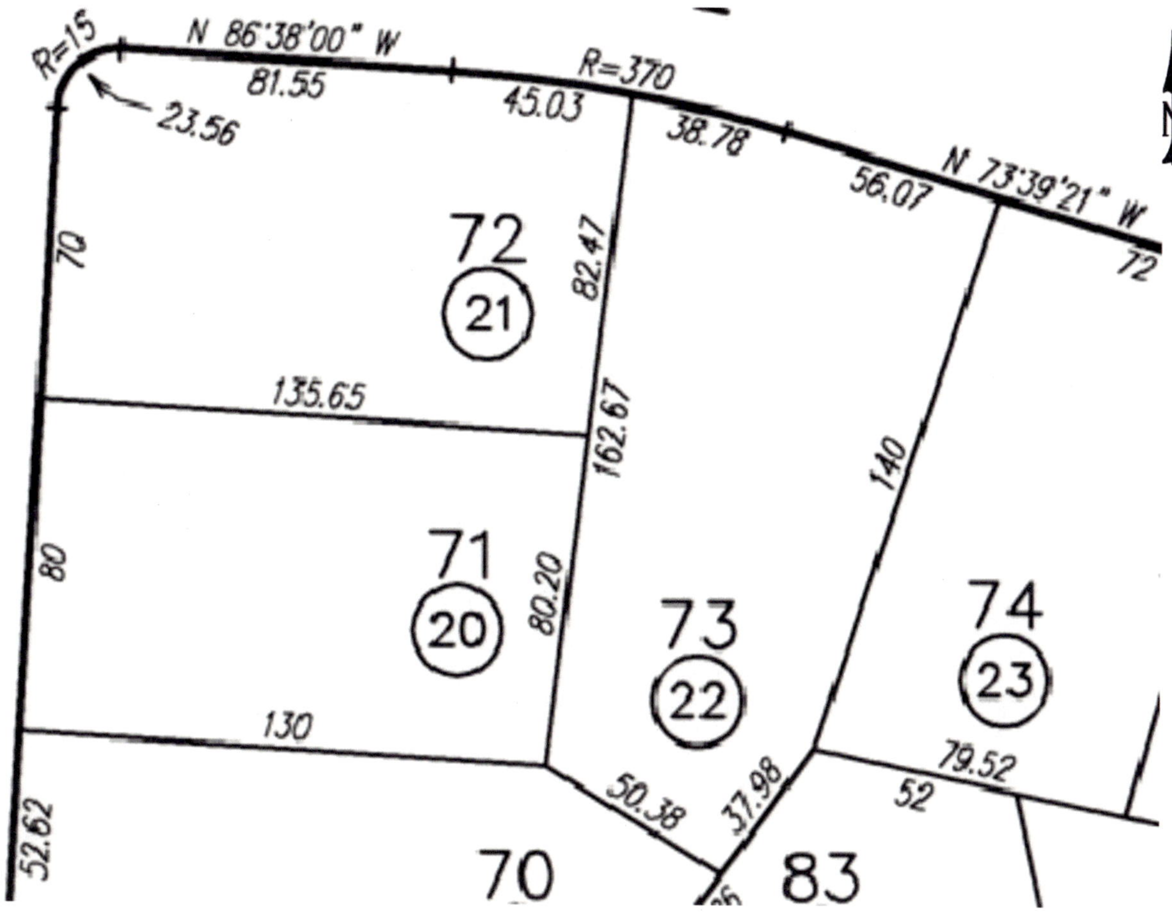

Suggested Steps

1.) Engineering UNITS, Precision 0'-0"; LIMITS: 170',240'; SNAP: 1'; GRID: 10'

2.) Copy and Paste image into AutoCAD (Hint: Print Screen and Paste into AutoCAD)

3.) Trace over the site image in AutoCAD with a LINE, then delete the site image

4.) Scale site to parcel map using the SCALE command with the Reference option

5.) Adjust lengths to match the map using PROPERTIES Palette, Grips, Object Snap, Osnap Tracking (Turn on Object Snap with Endpoint and Extension running object snaps)

6.) Join the site boundary lines into one object using the JOIN command

7.) Save the file as *ParcelMap-XXXXX.dwg* where XXXXX is the area in sq. ft. (Hint: PROPERTIES Palette)

PlantList

Introduction

In this assignment we will create a plant list for the existing backyard trees using the TABLE command.

Suggested Steps

1) Open the *TreesXX.dwg* drawing previously created
2) Go into the *Layout1* tab and delete the viewport
3) Create a new text STYLE, starting with the Standard style, named *StylusBT* that uses the Stylus BT font
4) Create a new TABLESTYLE called *Plantlist*
5) Modify the Cell Styles for the new table style as follows:

	Fill Color	Alignment	Margins	Text Style	Text Height
Title	Green	Middle Center	0.08" (H&V)	StylusBT	0.25
Header	None	Middle Center	0.06" (H&V)	StylusBT	0.18
Data	None	Middle Center	0.06" (H&V)	StylusBT	0.15

6) Using the *Plantlist* table style, create a new TABLE with 6 columns, 13 rows, and a 1.5" column width
7) Adjust the column widths using grips as needed to match the widths shown below

Plant List					
SYMBOL	TYPE	QTY	COST	EXTD COST	REMARKS
TBD	Juniper	3	$50.00	$150.00	2 Removed
TBD	Sago Palm	1	$350.00	$350.00	
TBD	Orange Tree	1	$225.00	$225.00	
TBD	Peach Tree	1	$350.00	$350.00	
TBD	Lime Tree	1	$100.00	$100.00	Small & Sick
TBD	Avocado Tree	1	$225.00	$225.00	
TBD	Ficus Tree	2	$125.00	$250.00	
TBD	Queen Palm	2	$300.00	$600.00	Not Shown
TBD	Bougainvilleeae	1	$75.00	$75.00	
TBD	Roshbushes	20	$20.00	$400.00	
	Totals	33	$1820.00	$2725.00	

8) Create and apply a new LAYER named *Text*
9) Complete the table data entry with the values shown above inserting sum formulas as needed
10) Save the file as *PlantListXX.dwg* where *XX* is your initials

myPhone3Plot

Introduction

In this assignment you will create an A-size and B-size plot layout of the myPhone3 drawing. The plot layouts will make use of your previous work in the *MyPhone3* and *TitleTemp* files.

Suggested Steps

1) Open the *TitleTempXX.dwg* file previously created

2) INSERT the drawing file *myPhone3XX.dwg* into the Model tab on *Objects* layer

3) Reposition and resize the viewports and objects in A-Size Layout and B-Size Layout as needed

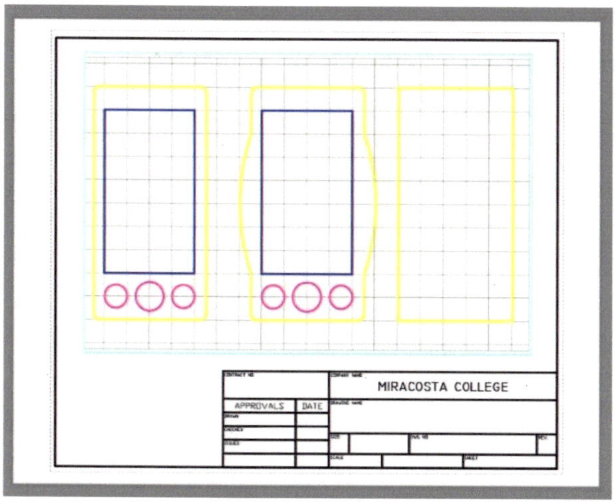

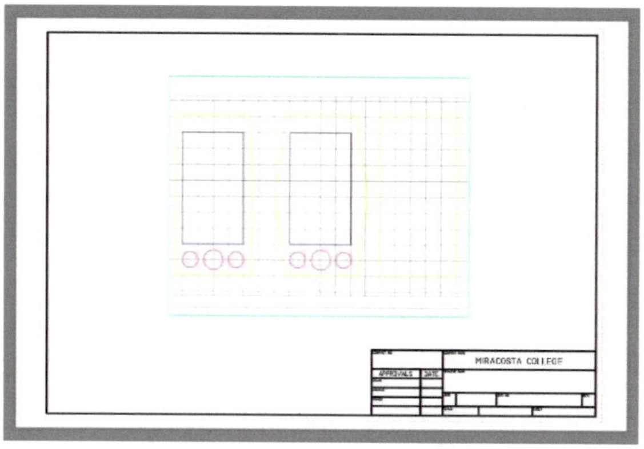

4) Turn off plotting in the *Vport* LAYER

5) Preview the PLOT for both layouts

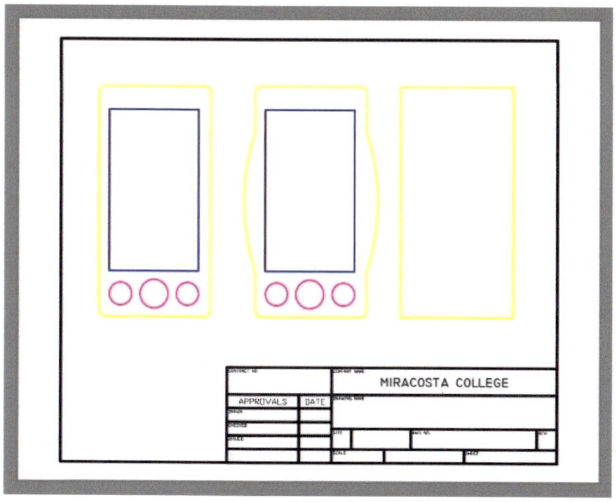

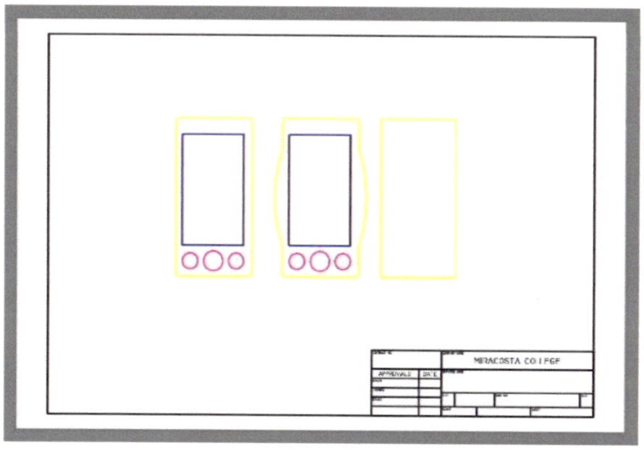

5) Save the file as *myPhone3PlotXX.dwg* where *XX* is your initials

myPhoneMVdims

Introduction

In this assignment you will INSERT a previously created drawing of the myPhone into the mechanical template and dimension the drawing. You will also adjust the location, size, and scale of the viewports in the layouts in preparation for plotting the layouts.

Suggested Steps

1) Open the *TitleTempXX.dwg* file previously created

2) INSERT the drawing file *myPhoneMV-XX.dwg* into the Model tab and EXPLODE it

3) Change the color of the *Button* and *Object* LAYERs to *blue*

4) Create the dimensions shown below on the *Dims* layer using the default *Standard* dimension style

5) Edit the dimensions with grips as needed and turn off unneeded extension lines with the PROPERTIES Palette

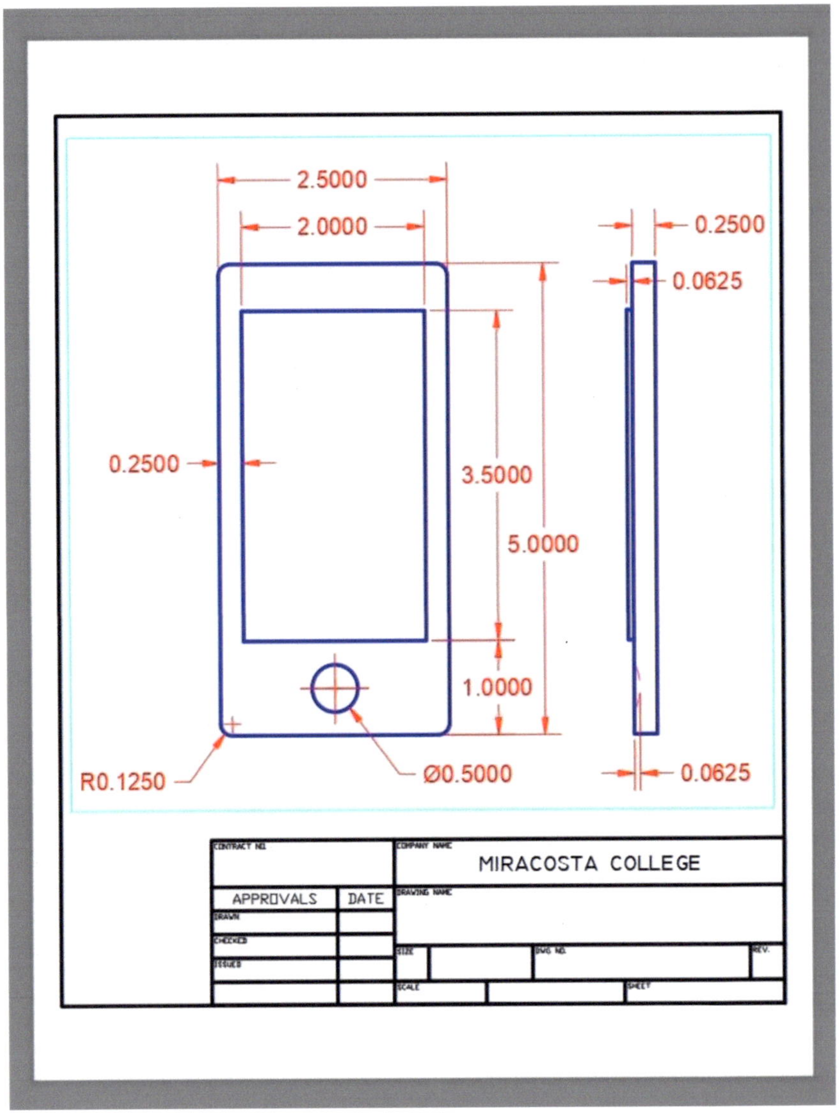

6) Resize and MOVE the viewports on the layouts to best display the viewports in each of the three layouts

7) Set the viewport scale to 1:1

8) Preview the PLOT of the three layouts

9) Save the file as *myPhoneMVdimsXX.dwg* where *XX* is your initials

Questions

Is the top view of this drawing needed? Why or why not?

Which of the layouts do you think is best for plotting this drawing?

ElevDimsMS

Introduction

In this assignment you will create a new dimension style for the house elevation drawing and use the dimension style to create dimensions in model space.

Suggested Steps

1) Open the drawing file *TitleblockEV-XX.dwg*

2) Change the UNITS Precision to 1/16" (this allows the dimensions style settings finer adjustments)

3) Create a new DIMSTYLE, starting with *Standard*, named *ModelDim* that has the following tab settings:

- *Lines*: Dimension lines and Extension lines *ByLayer*
- *Symbols and Arrows*: Arrowheads to Architectural tick, Arrow size 3/16"
- *Text*: New text style named *DimText* with Arial font; Text color ByLayer and Text height 1/4"
- *Fit*: Scale for dimension features Use overall scale of 48
- *Primary Units*: Linear dimensions Unit format to Architectural with a Precision of 0'-0"

4) Use the new *ModelDim* dimension style on the *Dimensions* layer to create the dimensions shown

5) Save your drawing as *ElevDimMS-XX.dwg* where *XX* is your initials

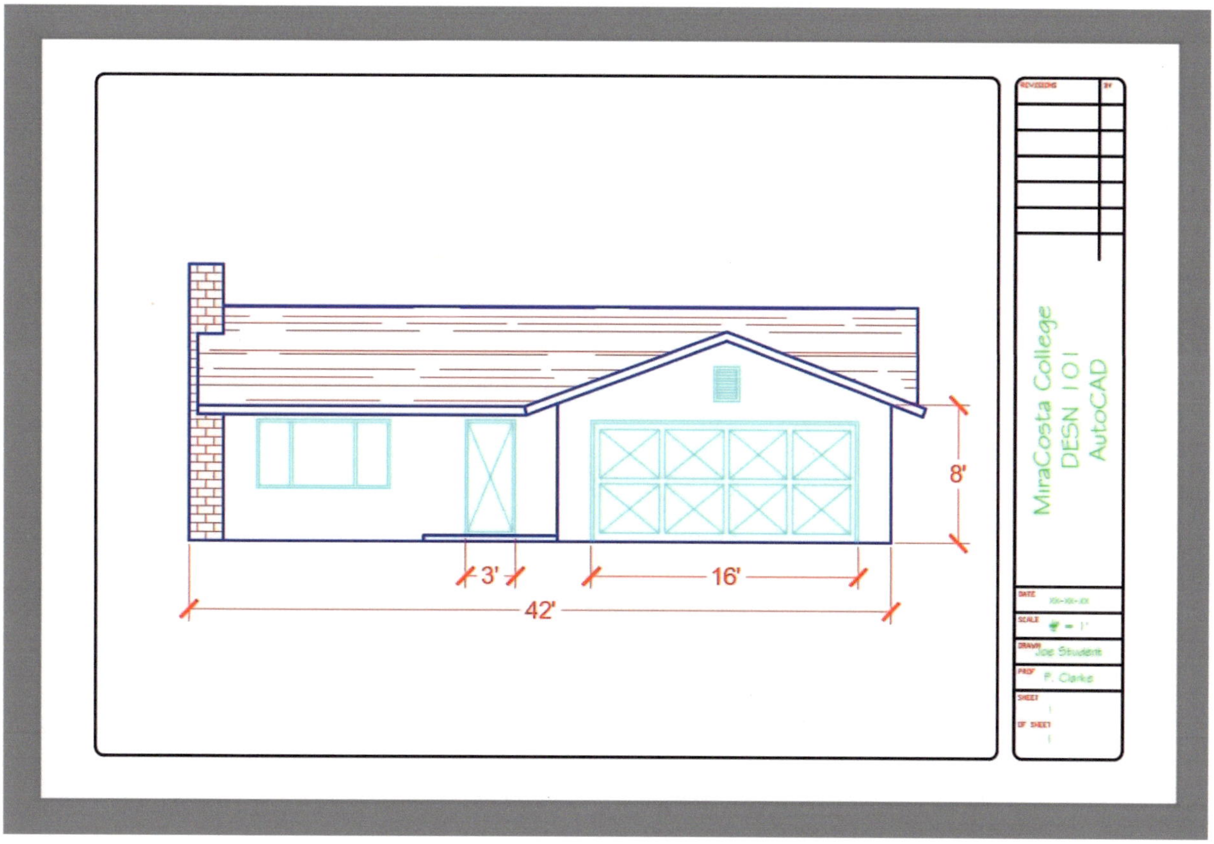

ElevDimsPS

<u>Introduction</u>

In this assignment you will create and plot a Layout tab with three viewports at three different scales showing different features dimensioned using a standard dimension style in paper space.

<u>Suggested Steps</u>

1) Open the file *ElevDimMS-XX.dwg* and delete the dimensions; delete the viewport in the Layout1
2) Create a new PAGESETUP, using the *Page Setup Manager,* called *B-Size Layout* with these settings:
   - Printer/plotter Name: AutoCAD PDF
   - Paper size: ANSI B (11.00 x 17.00 Inches)
   - What to plot: Layout
   - Set Current the *B-Size Layout* page setup
3) SCALE the title block and border down 1/48 and then cut and paste it to Layout1 using the Clipboard
4) Create a new DIMSTYLE called *PspaceDim* that starts with the *ModelDim* dimension style
   - From the Fit tab choose Scale dimensions to layout
5) Create new VIEWPORTS on the Viewports layer using the *Three: Below* standard viewport
6) Scale each viewport as follows: Garage Door 3/8"=1'0", Front Door ½"=1'0, Elevation 3/16"=1'
7) Resize the viewports (Paper Space), reposition the views (Model Space), and lock the viewports
8) Dimension the objects on the Dimensions layer in the three viewports in Paper Space as shown
9) Preview a PLOT with the Viewports LAYER set to not print
10) Save the drawing as *ElevDimPS-XX.dwg* where *XX* is your initials

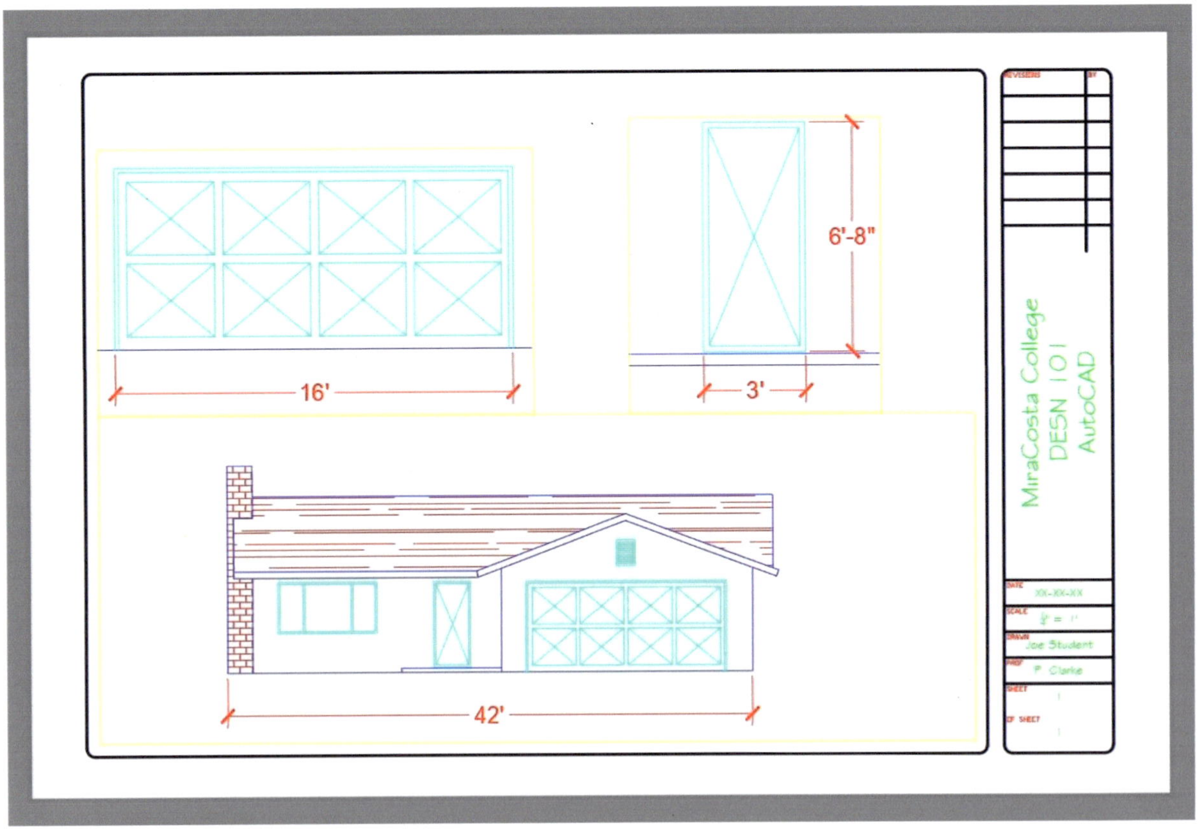

ElevDimAnno

Introduction

In this assignment you will create and use an annotative dimension style to dimension features in three different viewports at three different scales using dimensions in model space.

Suggested Steps

1) Open the drawing file *ElevDimsPS-XX.dwg*
2) Create a new annotative DIMSTYLE titled *AnnoDim:*
   - Start with the *PspaceDim* dimension style
   - Check the *Annotative* box in
   - Set *AnnoDim* as the Current dimension style
3) Delete the dimensions created in paper space
4) Dimension the three viewports in model space using the *Dimensions* layer
5) Observe how the dimensions appear in the Model tab versus Layout1 and consider why they differ
6) Observe what happens when you turn ANNOALLVISIBLE on and off by entering a value of 1 and 0
   Note you can also do this at the status bar by toggling *Show annotations objects* on and off.
7) Preview the PLOT of Layout1 and observe how it would look if plotted
8) Save the drawing file as *ElevDimAnnoXX.dwg* where *XX* is your initials

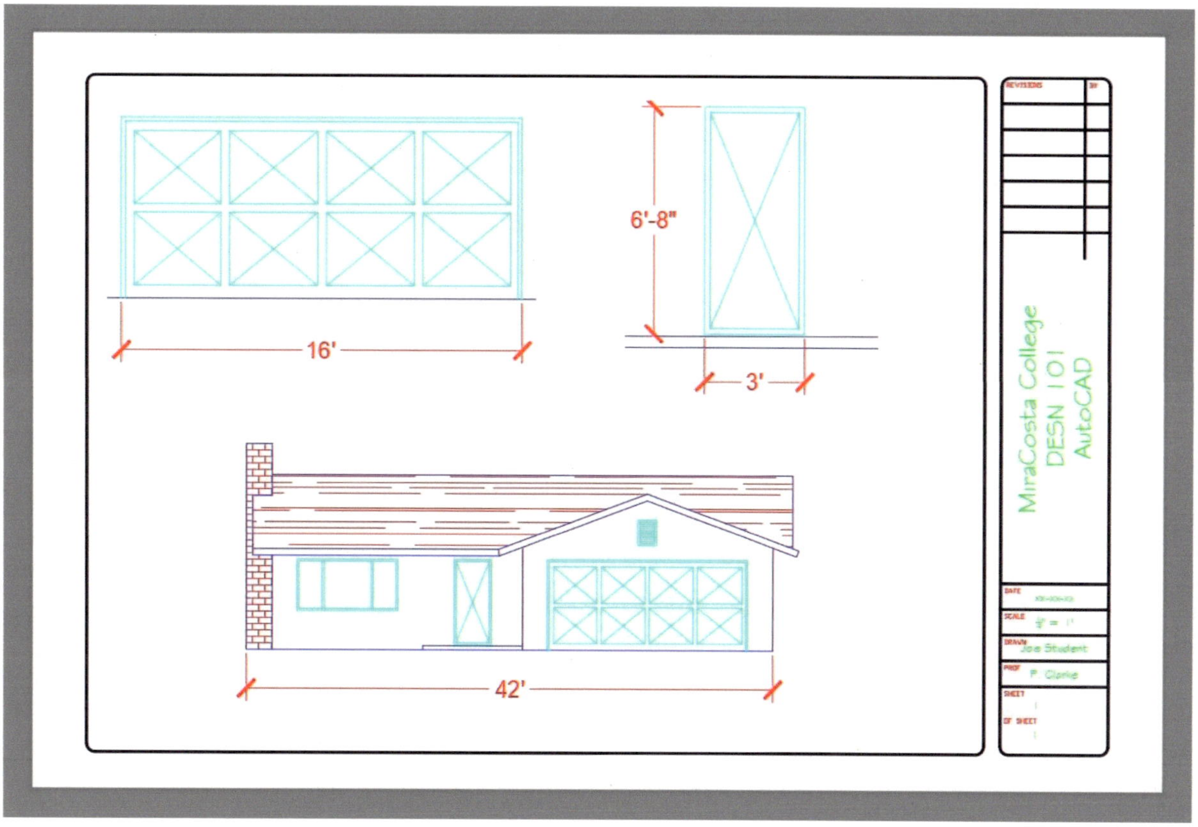

Polylines

Introduction

This is a fun assignment that will help you learn about the Polyline or PLINE command and some of the useful options within this command.

Instructions

Complete the shapes below using the acad.dwt template file and the PLINE command with the Width and Arc options. Use the grid to make the shapes proportionally similar, not to any exact size as dimensions are not given. The PEDIT command with the Fit and Spline options will also be useful. Save your work as *PolylinesXX.dwg* where *XX* is your initials.

Helpful Hints

The three polylines on the left side have a starting and ending Width of .2. The second and third polylines on the left are copies of the first, altered using PEDIT with the Fit and Spline options respectively.

The three polylines on the right side use different start and end Widths. The first polyline has a starting width of 0 and ending Width of 1, followed by starting and ending Widths of .2. The second and third polylines on the right use the Arc option. The third polyline begins with a start Width of 0 and end Width of .2, the end Width doubling with each additional segment.

LandLayout

<u>Introduction</u>

In this assignment you will use the landscape template to create a layout tab for a B-size sheet. You will also insert the landscape drawing into model space and copy the plant list table into the new layout.

<u>Suggested Steps</u>

1) Open the file *LandTempXX.dwg*
2) Rename the Layout1 tab *B-Size Layout*
3) Right click on *B-Size Layout* and select *Page Setup Manager*
4) Modify B-Size Layout as follows:
    - Printer/plotter Name: AutoCAD PDF
    - Paper size: ANSI B (11.00 x 17.00 Inches)
    - What to plot: Layout
5) Add and apply a custom Viewport Scale of 1" = 20' using SCALELISTEDIT with Scale properties 1=240 (note you can also right-click on Viewport Scale from the Status Bar and selecting Customize)
6) Resize the viewport to fit on *B-Size Layout* and INSERT the *PlantListXX.dwg* drawing into Model Space
7) COPYCLIP the table from *PlantListXX.dwg* and PASTECLIP into the *B-Size Layout*
8) Add a border, general notes, and title block on the appropriate layer, with the appropriate text style
9) Save the file as *LandLayoutXX.dwg* where *XX* is your initials

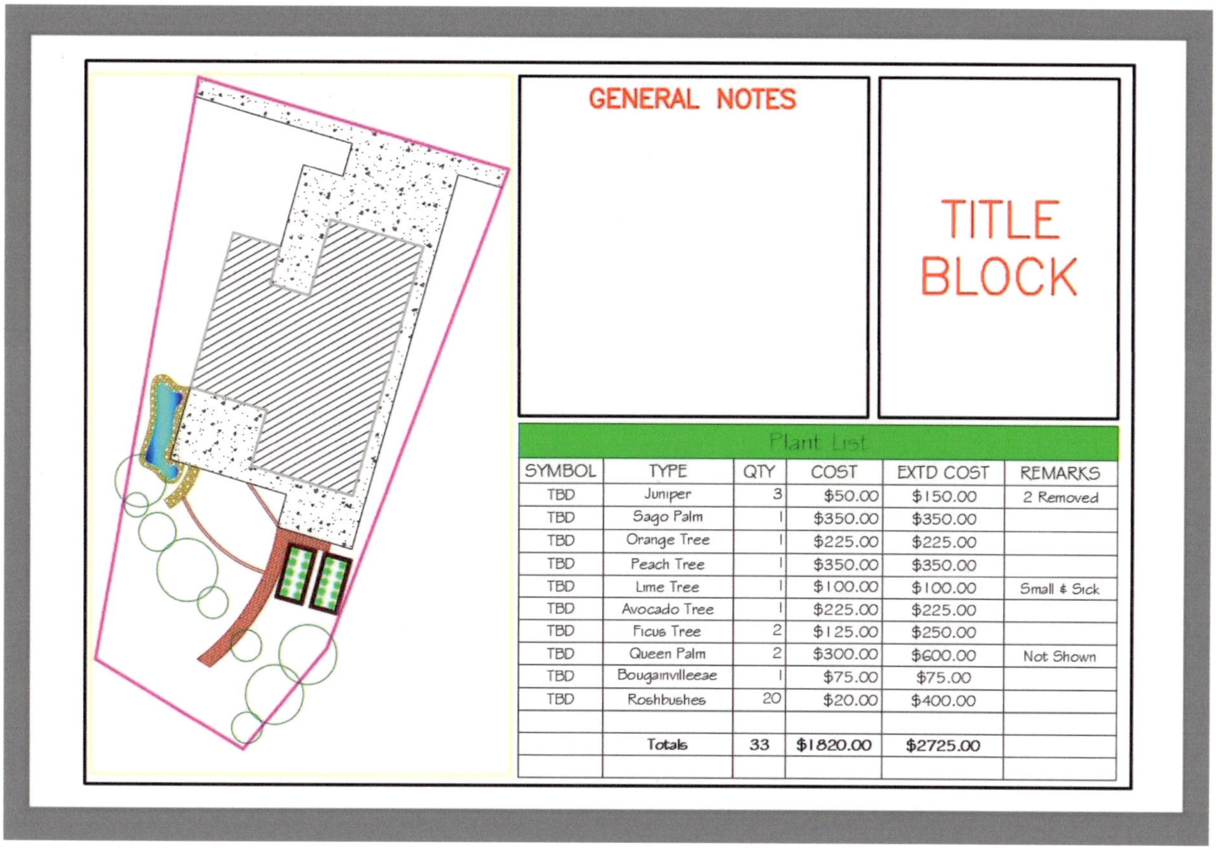

SYMBOL	TYPE	QTY	COST	EXTD COST	REMARKS
TBD	Juniper	3	$50.00	$150.00	2 Removed
TBD	Sago Palm	1	$350.00	$350.00	
TBD	Orange Tree	1	$225.00	$225.00	
TBD	Peach Tree	1	$350.00	$350.00	
TBD	Lime Tree	1	$100.00	$100.00	Small & Sick
TBD	Avocado Tree	1	$225.00	$225.00	
TBD	Ficus Tree	2	$125.00	$250.00	
TBD	Queen Palm	2	$300.00	$600.00	Not Shown
TBD	Bougainvilleeae	1	$75.00	$75.00	
TBD	Roshbushes	20	$20.00	$400.00	
	Totals	33	$1820.00	$2725.00	

Made in the USA
Monee, IL
12 November 2026

68261179R00029